why do **horses** sleep standing up?

why do **horses** sleep standing up **?**

101 of the Most Perplexing Questions Answered About Equine Enigmas, Medical Mysteries, and Befuddling Behaviors

Marty Becker, DVM
Audrey Pavia
Gina Spadafori
Teresa Becker

Health Communications, Inc.
Deerfield Beach, Florida

www.hcibooks.com

Library of Congress Cataloging-in-Publication Data

Why do horses sleep standing up? : 101 of the most perplexing
questions answered about equine enigmas, medical mysteries, &
befuddling behaviors / Marty Becker . . . [et al.] .

    p. cm.
  ISBN-13: 978-0-7573-0608-2 (trade paper)
  ISBN-10: 0-7573-0608-X (trade paper)
  1. Horses—Miscellanea. I. Becker, Marty, 1954–

SF285.W636 2007
636.1—dc22

2007020558

Publisher: Health Communications, Inc.
          3201 S.W. 15th Street
          Deerfield Beach, FL 33442–8190

Interior photos ©Photos.com, ©PhotoDisc
Cover design by Larissa Hise Henoch
Interior book design by Lawna Patterson Oldfield

Dedicated to the memory
of Barbaro, who showed us the
heart-pounding joy of victory,
the heartwarming spirit of hope,
and the heartbreaking
sadness of loss.

And in honor of Gretchen Jackson,
one of Barbaro's owners,
who put that loss in greater context
for us all, reminding us, always,
that grief is the price of love.

Contents

Foreword

Without the contribution of horses, you wouldn't be reading this book.

While the closest many of us get to a horse today is watching the Kentucky Derby or seeing a police horse do crowd control at a sporting event, the fact is that human civilization wouldn't have gotten very far without the contributions of the horse. They've done everything we've asked of them: served as beasts of burden, transportation, warrior, entertainer, and even, in some places, as dinner.

Now, of course, horses fill a role that's mostly recreational. Racehorses, show horses, trail partners, or oversized pasture ornaments: today we don't need horses to survive, but we still want them around. Perhaps this is because something in us always has and always will need what the horse symbolizes: freedom, beauty, strength, and speed.

Our past with horses hasn't always been advantageous from the horse's point of view. Horse training was more about "breaking" the animal, bending him to our will without regard to his needs and desires.

So much has changed and is continuing to change.

These days, training is increasingly about getting a horse to work "with" us instead of "for" us, and that takes knowledge, not just of what a horse can do and be made to do, but how a horse thinks and can learn to trust us. It's all about learning from the horse, listening to the horse, and moving forward together—about joining up, as I like to say.

My goal in life has always been to leave the world a better place than I found it, for horses and for people, too. The authors of this book—an award-winning team of horse lovers and experts—feel the same way. That's why I am happy to encourage you to settle in and enjoy the pages to follow.

You'll learn more about horses than you ever imagined possible, and you'll gain a better understanding and respect for one of humankind's oldest and most important partners. Join up, listen, learn, and have a laugh or two along the way. Life's a great ride, and we have horses to thank for it.

Monty Roberts
Author of *New York Times* bestseller
The Man Who Listens to Horses
www.montyroberts.com

Introduction

Not that long ago, you had no choice but to get along with horses. They pulled streetcars and carriages through our cities, took our young men and their munitions to war, pulled our plows and drays, and raced for our amusement. Every day, in every way, we relied on the horse. Whether you lived on a farm or in a city, chances are you saw horses every day.

Not so today, of course. Ever since we traded in the horse for the internal combustion engine, having a horse around is more of a luxury than a necessity. And yet, we just can't seem to get them out of our system.

Perhaps it's because they've been in our lives for so long. Our everyday language is packed with sayings that originate from horse lore: "long in the tooth," "getting a leg up," and many more. We even measure the power of the machines that replaced them in their namesake, with engines compared by horsepower, not oxpower or even manpower.

Or perhaps there's more to the story, to our seemingly eternal fascination with and connection to the horse. We are in awe of the horse, his beauty, speed, and strength. We marvel at his willingness to submit all of his gifts to our wishes and yet always remain true to himself. There is always something wild and free in every horse, and that surely appeals to us as well.

With this book we share our love of horses and our heartfelt desire to celebrate a bond that goes back through all recorded history. And we share, too, our love of sharing knowledge in a way that both entertains and informs.

Saddle up and read on. We're glad you're with us on this ride.

Dr. Marty Becker, Audrey Pavia,
Gina Spadafori, and Teresa Becker

Q: Why do horses sleep standing up?

A: *In the wild, when startled or alarmed,* animals survive through the fight-or-flight response. This is the same response that kicks in when someone jumps out from the dark and scares you: do you throw up your hands to fight, or do you engage your feet and take flight? Humans, who have been called the ultimate predators, often fight. Horses, who are in almost all situations prey (except for fights between horses), take flight.

By natural selection, horses who could sleep standing up, wake up, and run away from predators faster were the ones more likely to survive and pass on their genes. Put another way: when you're a large herbivore, and a carnivore with a rumbling stomach looks your way, you're better off if you can move at a moment's notice.

So that's why horses sleep standing up, but how do they do it? The answer is called a "stay apparatus," which is a unique adaptation of the musculoskeletal system of the horse that allows the animal to lock limbs in position so that very little muscle function is required to remain standing.

In the front legs, this is relatively easy, since these limbs naturally rest in a straight, load-bearing position. The hind legs presented a bigger challenge, however, and for them, horses have over time developed a combination of ligament and joint adaptations that allow them to lock two principle joints, the stifle and the hock, in a fixed and immovable position.

When enjoying a short nap, the horse will lock one hind limb in this fixed position. The weight of the hind end is resting on the locked limb while the other hind limb is in a flexed and resting position.

The stay apparatus is a nifty adaptation, but one small problem remains. Like humans, horses have both shallow sleep and a deeper period of rest known as rapid eye movement (REM) sleep. Horses need about fifteen minutes of REM sleep each day, and they can get that only while lying down. Good thing they don't need much REM sleep, because a horse who lies down for long periods of time has difficulty getting blood supply to the large muscles of the legs, which makes getting up difficult. The bigger the horse, the bigger the problem, which is why some horses (particularly the large draft horses) have a very difficult time recovering from lengthy periods under anesthesia.

Whether they are in the wild or in a domestic setting, a horse must feel safe before lying down to enjoy a few minutes of deep sleep. A horse would die without eventually getting deep sleep. There may be a delay of many hours, even days, but eventually a horse feels safe enough to go prone, go to the REM zone, and catch some deep z's. In a traditional herd setting, horses enjoy the protection of their herd during the time of deep sleep. Often one horse will stand and nap while the others lay down for a deep sleep.

Different horses require different amounts of deep sleep. Babies need more sleep than adults; fortunately, their mothers will protect them while they rest. Wild horses lie down less than domesticated horses. The difference is believed to be less about predators and more about the scarcity of food in the wild, which requires wild horses to eat pretty much day and night. Food isn't as much of a concern for most domesticated horses. The famous racehorse Seabiscuit, known for enjoying lots of deep-sleep naps, never had to worry about where his next meal was coming from, after all.

Getting a Leg Up

Horses are fast to run but slow to rise. Have you ever seen a horse get up? It's no easy feat. First they have to roll into a sitting position, tuck their hind legs under them, and stretch their front legs out in front. Then they slowly press their front half up into a sort of dog-sitting position. Then they swing their head as a counter-weight and push the back end up. So if a horse feels vulnerable, which most horses do when they're lying down, he'll sleep standing up.

Q: Why do horses let people ride them?

A: *Horses could easily dislodge humans* from their backs with an upward flick of their hind ends. So why don't they? The reason is actually pretty simple: horses recognize humans as dominant herdmates.

Horses are social animals who, in the wild, live in herds. And whenever there is a herd, there must be a leader, as well as a pecking order. Horses are good at figuring out who is in charge. It's part of their nature.

Domestic horses raised from a very young age by humans learn that people are the ones in charge. From the time they are born, these horses are taught to wear a halter, walk alongside a human, and move their feet the way people want them to. They are made to submit to human will from the get-go, so by the time they grow up, they see people as the dominant creatures in their world.

Horses trained for riding learn that humans like to climb up on their backs. There is no question in the horse's mind that he must submit to this idea, because, after all, these two-legged creatures are the ones in charge of everything.

Of course, some horses like to challenge the status quo, and some humans are better than others at establishing and maintaining dominance. Some humans won't allow horses to buck them off; some horses won't allow humans to ride them and will buck them off without a moment's notice. In some cases, these horses become professional rodeo broncos and end up making their living removing riders from their backs. So in the end, the humans still get what they want.

Q: Why do horses get spooked so easily?

A: *This is one of those age-old* questions often asked by those new to horses, as well as more experienced riders entering middle age—you know, that age when falling off a horse suddenly feels like a very big deal.

On the surface, it seems absurd that an animal as big as a horse would be afraid of anything, let alone a fluttering piece of paper. Yet most horses are real scaredy-cats, easily frightened by objects they can't readily identify, especially if these things are moving.

The horse's nervous nature stems from a long history as a prey animal. Long before being domesticated, the horse was at the top of the large predators' dinner menu. Creatures the likes of saber-toothed tigers, wolves, and even prehistoric humans are all believed to have regularly dined on horses.

Given this reality, it's not hard to understand why horses are so flighty. Even though a lot of time has passed since they were stalked by Ice Age creatures, the horse's instinct to run first and ask questions later remains ingrained.

So what does a piece of paper blowing across the trail have in common with a saber-toothed tiger? domesticated horses haven't had the experience of living in the wild, where they learn to recognize modern-day predators like coyotes, wolves, and mountain lions. The result is that when our horses see something strange in their environment, they often assume it isn't safe and act instinctively.

There's also the issue of vision. Unlike humans, who have a flexible lens inside each eye that can rapidly adjust and focus on objects at various distances, the horse's lenses are mostly rigid, so the only way to focus on something that's too close or too far away for his particular focal distance is to move his head closer or farther away. When a horse is scared, that takes too much time. So horses use the general philosophy of run first, investigate later. On top of all that, the shape of their eyeball gives them excellent long-distance vision (for keeping an eye on the horizon for bogeymen), but up close things are not only out of focus, they're actually magnified. So, an 8 x 10 piece of fluttering paper that's magnified and out of focus and moving and making a rustling noise (not too unlike the sound of a cougar sliding through the brush) may quite logically seem like something that could actually do some damage.

Stampeding is part of this same intrinsic need to flee from danger, combined with the horse's intense herd instinct. Horses are social animals, and they find safety in numbers. All it takes is for one member of the herd to act frightened, and the entire group will respond in kind, assuming the one who is scared is feeling that way for good reason. If one member of the herd takes off in fear, the others will follow in that classic staple of any Western movie, the stampede.

SPOOKY BY NATURE

In my lifetime of riding horses, I have encountered the entire gamut of spookers. Frantic spookers, careful spookers, whirling spookers, and spookers-in-place. I've ridden spookers who bolted and had to be pulled to a stop using an emergency one-rein maneuver. I've had spookers who jumped straight up in the air, landing exactly in the same spot where they were before they spooked. I've ridden horses who spooked at garbage trucks, waving flags, goats, and even miniature horses.

My very first spooker was a little bay mare named Peggy. She was my first horse, and the perfect child's mount: she was calm, reliable, and nearly fearless. Whizzing cars, barking dogs, and flying plastic bags didn't phase her. But she did have an Achilles' heel: the dreaded calabaza bush. This terrifying flora lurked along the side of trails, hiding between darker foliage, trying to camouflage itself from unsuspecting horses. With their large pale leaves and their yellow-orange summer squash–like gourds, they were horrific and menacing—at least to Peggy—and only, it seems, when we were galloping along on the trail while I was bareback and barefoot.

Peggy's modus operandi for spooking at top speed was to suddenly leap to the side as she passed a calabaza bush. Without a saddle to grab, I'd go flying off and land butt-first in the dirt. She'd stop and wait for me to climb back on until the next time we passed one of those green monsters.

These days, I'm a lot less cavalier about falling off a horse. I wear a helmet and riding boots, and always use a saddle. I also choose to ride horses who have a low spook threshold, since my idea of a fun ride isn't holding on for dear life over every sight and sound on the trail.

It's amazing how much horses vary from individual to individual when it comes to spookability. While a more daring rider may not mind constant jumpiness in an equine companion, I prefer a braver horse, one even braver than my old friend Peggy.

Audrey Pavia

Why do they measure horses in hands and what does it mean?

A: *Most horses weigh about* 1,000 to 1,200 pounds. But horse people don't consult the scales when describing how big their horses are, nor do they refer to the tape measure. Oddly, at least to nonhorse people, the size of a horse rests in the palm of the hand. You see, even in an age of laser accuracy where distances are measured with great precision, the standard measurement of a horse's height is still done in hands.

A hand is equal to 4 inches, with one-inch increments (1 inch being equivalent to .1 hands, 2 inches being equivalent to .2 hands, and so on), and horses are measured from the ground to the top of their withers, the high point of the back located between the shoulder blades. So if a horse measures 60 inches high, the horse is 15 hands. If the horse stands 62 inches off the ground, the horse is 15.2 hands. Because the hand is an increment of 4 inches, if the tape measure shows 64 inches, the horse is 16 hands, not 15.4 hands.

The story behind this unit of measurement is that a king went to measure his favorite horse. Not having a device to measure with, he used the only thing he knew would be consistent—the palm of his hand—which measured four inches across. Since then, the hand has been the unit of measure for equines.

Giving Yourself a "Hand"

Height is really only important if you intend to ride a horse or show it. An average woman does well with horses from 14 to 16 hands tall, whereas larger men may want to saddle up a horse 16 hands or more. Horse size has a lot to do with fashion as well as function. Just as great big guys can look a little funny shoehorned into tiny economy cars, a tall person looks better on a tall horse than on a tiny one. And if you're heavy, a larger horse can carry you more comfortably for a longer period of time than one whose back sags under your weight.

Q: How well do horses see?

A: *Horses see everything necessary* to avoid danger but don't see it terribly well. Human eyes are set in the front of our heads. This gives us binocular, stereoscopic vision, which means that our eyes combine the images we see to obtain a three-dimensional effect. This results in excellent depth perception, also shared by other hunters, such as dogs, cats, hawks, and owls. Horses, however, have eyes set on the sides of their heads, providing excellent lateral vision, a trait they share with other prey species, such as sheep, deer, rabbits, ducks, and pigeons.

The highly elastic lens we humans have allows us to change focus from near to far without moving our heads (if we're young and don't wear bifocals or trifocals). The horse's less-elastic lens requires altering the head position in order to focus.

Horses can't see that well directly in front of them, or directly behind either. This is one reason it's always a good idea to speak to a horse before approaching from behind. If the horse can't see you approaching, he may become startled and kick out in defense at whatever he senses is coming up on his rear.

The horse's visual acuity up close and in the middle distance isn't that great compared with humans. A horse needs to be standing twenty feet away from an object to see it as well as a human does at thirty-three feet. Horses see better than dogs and cats do, though. And they're great at seeing things across the pasture, especially when their heads are down in the grazing position, which puts the horizon right smack in the sharpest part of their retina.

When it comes to night vision, horses have humans beat. Many a trail rider who has stayed out past sunset has depended on a horse to get back home. It takes a horse about fifteen minutes for his eyes to adjust from light to dark conditions, but once that happens, a horse can see very well in starlight. Horses possess more rods in their eyes than humans do, and rods are needed for superior night vision.

Although horses see better than we do in the dark, their world is not as colorful as ours. Horses have similar vision to humans who are red-green color-blind. They can see most of the colors we do, but when it comes to red and green, they tend to see them only as gray. The colors they do see are rendered in pastel shades.

The different way horses see the world is highlighted in this clever warning for anyone who seeks to approach one:

> *Never approach a bull from the front,*
> *A horse from the rear,*
> *Or a fool from any direction.*

Q: **What is the biggest breed of horse?**

A: *Draft horses are the largest equines,* with many weighing nearly a ton and towering high above their human handlers. Among the draft breeds, the Shire is king when it comes to size. According to Guinness World Records, a Shire horse by the name of Samson holds the record as the largest horse ever. Born in England in 1846, Samson weighed 3,300 pounds and stood nearly 22 hands high at the withers—more than 7.5 feet tall at the shoulder!

Q: **What is the smallest breed of horse?**

A: *The smallest horse breed around is* the Falabella, an Argentinean breed of miniature horse that regularly measures 30 inches at the withers. The horse holding the record for being the smallest individual horse with the Guinness World Records is a miniature horse named Thumbelina. Born in 2001 in Missouri, Thumbelina stands only 17.5 inches high at the withers.

Q: Why are so many horses afraid to step into water?

A: Cats are the ones who are supposed to be afraid of water, yet many horses aren't far behind. Horses will stand quietly for a bath delivered by a garden hose, yet they will balk when asked to step into even the most innocuous puddle.

The reason for the equine aversion to water is simple: horses don't have much in the way of depth perception when something is directly in front of them. Because their eyes are located on the sides of their heads, they have monocular vision, which renders their close-up front view virtually two-dimensional. Monocular vision is very handy for horses when it comes to seeing what is happening on both sides of the body, but it's not very helpful when trying to get a sense of the depth of bodies of water.

When a rider directs a horse to step into a puddle, creek, river, or lake, the horse is being asked to take a huge leap of faith. The horse has no idea how deep the water is, and for all she knows, she is going to sink deep into a watery chasm if she sets foot in the wet stuff.

A horse must have considerable trust in her rider to step into water. This trust may come through having many experiences being ridden through water without incident or may simply be the result of a very strong bond with her rider.

Horses who are afraid to step into water can be gradually taught that puddles and rivers are safe. If a horse sees another equine go into the water first and survive, she will know it's fine to follow.

Q: What is the strongest breed of horse?

A: *The strongest horses are the draft breeds.* Bred specifically for hauling heavy objects (like logs), these horses can pull with incredible force. The Belgian in particular is one of the strongest of the draft breeds. In fact, a team of two Belgians can pull as much as 4,500 pounds without a problem.

Q: What's the difference between a foal, a colt, and a filly?

A: *A foal is a baby horse of either gender.* A colt is a young male horse, from birth until the age of three. A filly is a young female horse, from birth until the age of three. At maturity, male horses are either stallions or geldings (the latter if castrated), while females are mares. When mares enter a breeding program, they're called broodmares. When broodmares are pregnant, they're said to be "in foal." When they're delivering their babies, it's called "foaling."

Many people use the word "colt" to describe a newborn baby horse, but of course, that's only right if the baby's a boy. If you see baby horses in the field with their moms, you'll sound like you know what you're talking about if you refer to them all as foals until you can determine otherwise!

Q: **How long does it take for a baby horse to learn to stand?**

A: *Foals are the junior athletes* of the animal world. Unlike kittens and puppies, young horses are able to walk, and even run, shortly after birth. In fact, within an hour or two of exiting the womb, baby horses are on their feet and nursing. By the *second hour,* a newborn foal can run after Mom at a gallop. And in the wild, he'll have to. The afterbirth, birth fluids, and the newborn foal himself are odorless at birth. This is to help protect him from predators while he and Mom are vulnerable. But it doesn't take long for the discarded tissues to start taking on a dis-stink-tive fragrance, and for the foal to develop enough of a smell signature to leave a scent trail that any self-respecting predator could follow. So, as soon as he's relatively steady on his feet, and while things are still nasally neutral, Mom takes the newly standing baby a mile or two away from the birthing place, usually at a pretty good clip.

While foals get their feet under them much more quickly than many other baby animals, standing is still a challenging endeavor for a newborn horse. Foals have incredibly long legs that seem to be made of rubber when the babies are first trying to stand. The legs bend this way and that as the poor foal teeters gingerly in an attempt to balance. But this awkwardness doesn't last for long, and usually within a couple of hours, the youngster has a pretty good grip on how to use those spindly appendages.

Foals are much quicker getting on their feet than other animals because horses are prey animals. In the wild, they are on the menu of large predators, such as mountain lions, wolves, and coyotes. Because full-grown horses are hard to take down, even for formidable predators like mountain lions (horses can kick!), baby horses are the preferred meal.

For foals to survive in the wild, they need to be able to get to their feet quickly, take in nourishment from their mothers' milk as soon as possible, and run like the dickens in a short period of time. Without this ability to stand and flee soon after birth, not many foals would get a chance to grow up in the wild.

Q: **What's up with all the sayings about a horse's mouth: "straight from the horse's mouth," "long in the tooth," and "don't look a gift horse in the mouth"? Why all the interest in what's inside a horse's mouth?**

A: You can tell a lot by looking inside a horse's mouth, and that's the basis for the origins of all these phrases. Here's more, straight from the . . . well, you know.

One explanation is that the phrase "straight from the horse's mouth" comes from the racetrack. In the early decades of the twentieth century, horse racing was considered one of the top spectator sports in the United States, along with boxing and baseball. Betting was one of the reasons why. Before putting down any money, any horseplayer worth his salt would try to get a peek inside the horse's mouth, or talk to someone who claimed to have done so, giving the gambler the edge on knowing the horse's true age and condition. Horseplayers these days are more likely to judge a horse by his breeding and past performances than by his dentistry, but the colorful phrase remains in wide use to describe accurate information from those in the know.

The other explanation relates directly to horse traders, the proverbial used car salespeople of the day. A horse trader would bend the ear of a prospective buyer with all kinds of talk about the horse's pedigree, age, health, strength, stamina, and breeding capability, all with an eye to selling at the highest price possible. If a horse trader bragged about a horse's age and condition, well, maybe it was true and maybe it was not. To cut through the hyperbole and get a quick measure of the horse's true condition and worth, a savvy buyer could simply look in the horse's mouth for a good read of the animal's age, health, and even behavior—if a horse was so unruly he had to be reined in a lot, this, too, would show up in the mouth.

Of course, age is one of the primary things that can be pretty accurately "guesstimated" with a look in a horse's mouth. A horse's gums recede with age, exposing more of the root and making the teeth appear longer. "Long in the tooth" has come to mean old age, in general terms, whether you're talking about a horse or a TV set.

Now, what about that "gift horse" you shouldn't be "looking in the mouth"? It's an age-old adage about minding your manners. When someone gives you something, it's rude to question its value, which is exactly what you'd be doing if you looked in the mouth of a horse someone gave you.

Showing that manners have been important for many generations, some version of the "gift horse" phrase has been used since around AD 400, with versions in Latin as well as English, French, German, Italian, and Spanish.

Q: **Why do flies like horses so much?**

A: *The fly is the bane of every horse's* (and horse owner's) existence. These annoying insects drive horses crazy, getting into their eyes, biting their legs, and crawling on their bellies. If you've seen horses standing around swishing their tails relentlessly, it's because flies are bugging the heck out of them.

Flies like—no, love!—horses so much because these creepy bugs evolved over time to make a living off large plant-eating animals such as the horse. All kinds of flies are out there, each with its own pesky specialty. For instance, the face fly feeds on secretions from the horse's eye. The stable fly draws blood from the horse's legs. The horsefly sucks blood from the horse's upper body, and the blackfly feeds on blood from the inside of the horse's ears.

Some flies prefer to borrow the horse's digestive system as a way of reproducing. Botflies lay their eggs on the horse's front legs, belly, or hind legs and wait for the horse to accidentally ingest them when scratching himself with his teeth (no opposable thumbs available for such things).

Once the eggs get into the horse's mouth, they hatch, burrow for a time inside the cheeks and gums, then drop down and attach themselves to the lining of the stomach. Eventually they detach, go through a cocoonlike stage, and emerge as botflies and start the entire yucky process over again.

Houseflies, on the other hand, like to lay their eggs directly in the horse's manure, where they hatch, feed, and turn into annoying adult flies. These are the little buggers you see the most when you hang around horses. These disgusting poop-eaters are everywhere.

Flies are such a big problem for horses and their owners that an entire industry has sprung up to deal with them. Scores of companies produce fly sprays, roll-ons, and wipes, all designed to keep flies off the poor, suffering equine. One company even makes a food additive that horse owners can put in their horses' grain to keep fly larvae from developing into adults in the horse's manure.

But the fly wars don't stop there. Special fly control systems rigged up to barn ceilings are designed to periodically spray insecticide on the horses below to keep flies from settling, biting, and laying. And if all this wasn't enough, "horse clothing" manufacturers have created a slew of protective apparel to cover horses from head to toe to protect them from the onslaught of biting flies.

Unfortunately for horses, flies are like cockroaches: they have survived the millenniums and will probably always be here. Although technology will continue to search for ways to annihilate the horse-loving fly, frequent cleaning of horse poop will remain the most tried and true method of keeping these irritating insects at bay. To augment that effort, the most earth-friendly (and arguably the most effective) way to control flies is to release tiny bugs (fly predators) that eat the larvae (maggots) that hatch from the eggs the female flies lay in the horse manure. Such predators are naturally present in the environment, but they don't reproduce as efficiently as flies do, so the flies maintain the upper hand unless you boost the predators' population. And unfortunately all the insecticide sprays that get used at horse facilities to kill flies also kill the fly predators and ultimately make the fly problem worse.

Q: How do you take a horse to the veterinarian?

A: *A horse won't fit in a portable carrier,* and you can't shove him into the backseat of your car. Not every horse owner has a horse trailer. That means when it comes to caring for horses, the veterinarian is usually the one who travels.

Most equine veterinarians have mobile practices. These veterinarians carry their offices with them on their "barn calls," and have pickup trucks or SUVs specially equipped to hold the tools they need. They have a small refrigerator for drugs that need to be kept cool, and compartments for needles, syringes, and bandages. Some carry handheld X-ray machines, while others have portable ultrasound equipment. Equine veterinarians also keep a huge variety of medications and other tools on hand to help them diagnose and treat sick horses.

Because horses are such big animals and are hard to transport, equine vets often find themselves in situations where they must perform certain procedures right in the horse's stall. Many a horse has been stitched up, heavily bandaged, and even castrated without ever having set foot outside the barn.

While many horse illnesses and injuries can be treated "in the field," a good many do require a trip to the horse hospital in a trailer. In certain parts of the country, owners can call an "equine ambulance," which is equipped with a hydraulic system to load a horse that can't stand.

Equine hospitals are specially equipped to handle horse patients and feature surgical tables large enough to accommodate a 1,000-pound animal. They also have lifts to get the horse onto the table, and padded rooms or pools for horses to stay in while they are coming out of anesthesia. (A horse waking up from surgery can thrash, stumble, and fall numerous times, which is why the walls and floor are padded, or the horse is placed on a raft with legs hanging down into the water.)

Horse hospitals also feature special stalls where horses receive round-the-clock care. The attending veterinarians make their rounds every morning, just like doctors do in a human hospital. Patients are attended to constantly by veterinary technicians, the nurses of the animal world.

In case you are wondering who pays the bill when a

horse gets sick, it's usually the owner, unless the horse happens to be insured. Yes, medical insurance is available for horses, and believe or not, it's far more affordable than human health insurance these days.

A SPECIALIST FIT FOR A HORSE, OF COURSE

When horse owners gets into a pinch—whether with a medical concern or just the challenges of grooming, training, or doctoring an unpredictable horse—they often wish they had the training, experience, and confidence of an equine veterinarian.

So do I—and I *am* a veterinarian!

My late father, Bob, had been seriously injured by a horse when he was very young, and it seems he transferred his rabid fear of horses to me. In veterinary school, many of the horses we treated were Thoroughbreds fresh from the racetrack, and they would eat the lunch of every veterinary student who was quaking in their boots—that would be me and about two-thirds of my classmates to a lesser degree. The other third thought of horses as golden retrievers with hooves and could communicate with and handle them as such.

My dreams of being able to handle horses with

aplomb in front of my horse-loving family at our horse ranch in northern Idaho was put to the test one summer day.

As I stood leaning over the corral fence with my son Lex, who was then eleven, I told him, "When I get inside I need to call the veterinarian to come vaccinate our horses, worm them, and float their teeth."

"Let me get this straight, Dad," Lex replied incredulously. "You're a famous veterinarian but you have to call another vet to come out and take care of the horses? Why?"

"Lex, you see our quarter horse, Chex, over there?"

"Yeah, I see him, Dad,"

"Well, Lex, he's a lot bigger and faster than I am. And to tell you the truth, I'm a little scared of horses, especially when I am doing something to them that might scare them or cause them discomfort."

What I was really thinking was that Chex was a potential ninja with hooves. Chex weighs more than a half a ton, has long legs powered by bulging muscles that can almost instantly accelerate him to speeds of more than thirty miles per hour, and has legs tipped by rock-hard hooves that can do a tap dance on your feet or face faster than a boxer on amphetamines. On top of that, a brain the size of a grape powers this potentially lethal machine.

Fast-forward to the day the local veterinarian, Dr. Rolan Hall, or as everyone knows him locally, Toad, arrived to treat the horses. Our whole family was out there to greet him.

Toad is a legend in Boundary County, Idaho, which is pinched between Washington and Montana, like the tip of a finger pressing against the Canadian border. A muscular man with a booming voice, he has maintained most of the body that made him a wrestling superstar in high school. Oh, yeah, and did I mention that he used to be one of my wife's old boyfriends? And that he isn't scared of horses?

As soon as Toad's truck pulled up to the corral, the horses' eyes widened with fear, nostrils flared, and muscles rippled like a can of worms. These horses were under attack from a predator—the vet—and their instinct to run was being blocked by the five wooden rails of the corral fence At least, that is how it seemed to me. In reality, they were just a bit excited by the change in the routine and the anticipation that something different was about to happen.

Still, excited horses can look pretty scary to an equine neophyte like me.

I watched from the safety of the outside of the fence as one by one, Toad began to give them the veterinary equivalent of a lube, oil, and filter. Powerful Pegasus, the biggest and most dominant of our horses, reared when Toad delivered the intranasal vaccine. As Pegasus rose, Toad one-handedly rode the horse's halter up and pulled him back to earth with a hand the size of a base-ball mitt. Gabriel, the giant palomino, swung his head violently to the side while having his teeth filed down (or so it seemed to me), striking Toad with a glancing blow on the side of the head and covering the left side of his face in a mixture of horse saliva and blood that typically follows rou-tine equine dentistry. Toad shook this off like minor inconveniences while I stood cowering behind the fence, safely out of harm's way.

I watched my horse-crazy wife, Teresa, marvel at the veterinarian's skill with horses. My daughter, Mikkel, who's expressed interest in being a veterinarian, was asking him questions about this as a career choice. And Lex kept saying over and over, "Toad's not scared of horses at all, Dad!"

As though I needed reminding. About this time, I was feeling around six inches tall instead of my regular six feet.

To make matters worse, at the end of Toad's visit to our Almost Heaven Ranch, he went to his truck and got out some homemade horse treats, came up to the fence where we were standing, and gave each of the horses an irresistible yummy and gently rubbed the back of his hand against their muzzles.

Heck, now even the horses worshipped him.

In reality, this was a scary event for me, but nobody else was concerned. Not Teresa, the family, Toad, or the horses. Just like those students with horse sense and savvy in veterinary school, Toad was the hero, and I was still a zero. At least when it came to horses.

Dr. Marty Becker

Q: What is the fastest breed of horse?

A: The fastest breed of horse over a distance of a mile or more is the Thoroughbred, a breed developed in England. The great Thoroughbred stallion Secretariat set a world record for running one and a half miles in two minutes and twenty-four seconds at the 1973 Belmont Stakes, which experts believe may never be broken.

The fastest breed of horse at less than a mile is the Quarter Horse. These horses, bred for sprinting, can easily run a quarter of a mile in twenty-two seconds flat.

Q: Do horses get claustrophobic when riding in trailers?

A: Horses are like people when it comes to traveling. Some enjoy it and some don't. The trick is to convince a horse that getting into and riding in a trailer is not a bad thing.

Because they are prey animals, horses are naturally claustrophobic. Being confined and unable to flee at will is nerve-racking stuff for an animal who has survived for millions of years by running away from danger.

So given this reality, how do people get horses into trailers? Not by forcing them, that is for sure. You can't force 1,000 pounds of muscle into a tin can on wheels no matter how hard you try. Instead, you teach the horse that being inside the trailer is a good thing.

Training to load and ride in a trailer begins at a very young age for most horses. Some have their first trailer ride alongside their moms. Others are taught to load into a trailer when they are one or two years old. This is done in gradual steps, where the horse is coaxed into the trailer and rewarded with food for standing quietly.

Occasionally, horses have bad experiences in trailers or are not properly taught to load and ride in a trailer. Horses who won't load can be quite a handful when it comes time to get into the trailer. Horses who freak out once inside are a disaster waiting to happen. The horse can seriously hurt himself (and other horses in the trailer) as he struggles to break free. That's why horse owners who travel with their horses regularly stop and check on their equine passengers, just to make sure everyone is having a smooth, safe ride.

Q: **Why do domesticated horses wear horseshoes if wild horses can cope without them?**

A: Horseshoes have been around for almost 2,000 years. Since the twelfth century or before, these shoes were made of iron. The express purpose of iron shoes is to protect the bottom of the horse's hoof from wear and tear.

Controversy rages in the horse world over whether horses should or should not wear shoes. Believers in the "barefoot method" say the horse's hoof is good enough as it is and should not be marred by an iron shoe.

It's true that wild horses manage very well without shoes. Barefoot trimmers say this is because these horses live in an ideal environment for horse's hooves. These horses eat a lot of roughage, move constantly as they graze, toughen their feet by traveling on a variety of surfaces, and regularly wet their hooves by standing in mud or shallow water as they drink from creeks, wells, and ponds.

Domestic horses, on the other hand, live in small stalls where their movement is restricted, eat food that is richer than what wild horses eat, and rarely get their feet wet. The result? Dry, brittle, tender feet that need shoes to protect them. Advocates of horseshoes claim that domesticated horses are asked to work a lot harder than wild horses, being made to trot, canter, and gallop much more often than a wild horse would.

Those who choose to keep their horses in shoes usually have a farrier come out every four to eight weeks to trim the hooves and put on new shoes. For racehorses, shoes can be changed even more frequently, depending on the conditions of the racetrack and the special needs of the racehorse.

Strange as it may seem, when a farrier applies a hot shoe and nails it into place, it doesn't hurt the horse. The material that makes up the outer part of the horse's hoof is a lot like our own fingernails. No nerve endings can be found in the areas where the hot shoe is laid down and where the nails are hammered. However, farriers have to be careful how they set the nails. If a nail goes in at the wrong angle, it can hit the interior area of the hoof containing nerves and cause the horse to become lame.

Q: Do horses have good memories?

A: *Do they ever!* They seem to remember everything that happens to them. That's one reason they are so trainable. What you teach a horse today, he will remember tomorrow. The more you reinforce it, the more it will stay in his memory until finally, it will be ingrained for life.

The great equine memory is one reason older horses tend to make such wonderful riding companions. All the experience they have gleaned stays with them. They remember things, such as trash cans on the side of the trail are harmless and people often hand out carrots. They also remember that behaving well while being ridden pleases the rider. Just like humans, horses digest and remember the encounters they have, good or bad, and add them to their life experiences.

Of course, this terrific equine memory can backfire on humans. If a horse has a bad experience, he remembers it. And then you have to spend a lot of time trying to get him to forget it.

Q: What's the difference between a pony and a horse?

A: The most obvious difference between a horse and a pony is size. Horses are generally bigger than ponies. Most horse breed registries consider equines below 14.2 hands at the withers to be ponies. True ponies are also proportioned differently than horses. Compare a Shetland's build, for example, to that of a miniature horse. Ponies are thicker through the body compared to their height than horses are and tend to have higher-stepping leg action.

But like most things in life, it's not that simple. Equines can be found who are less than 14 hands in height yet have the word "horse" in their name—not "pony." One example of this is the Icelandic Horse, an ancient breed developed in Iceland (of course) that only measures 12.3 to 13.1 hands. No word exists in Icelandic for "pony," so the breed is referred to as the Icelandic Horse.

The Norwegian Fjord Horse is another example. Individuals in this breed sometimes measure less than 14

46

hands, which would make them ponies by most definitions. Yet those who keep this breed consider all members of the breed to be horses.

Despite this confusing breed nomenclature, it's safe to say that any small horse under 14.2 hands in height is a pony. Examples of ponies without question are the Shetland Pony, Welsh Pony, and Pony of the Americas.

Q: Are some breeds better at long-distance riding than others?

A: Since America was young, horses have been ridden very long distances over short periods of time. Early explorers, such as Lewis and Clark, put many miles on the horses they rode during the mounted parts of their journey. Pony Express riders sprinted 15 miles at a gallop to complete each segment of their route as they delivered the mail.

Racing horses long distances has been an American sport for centuries, too. In 1893, a 1,000-mile horse race was conducted from Chadron, Nebraska, to Chicago. The winner took home $1,000—a lot of money back then—and received publicity all throughout the country.

Horses in general are capable of traveling 100 miles in a day. However, it's not something that every individual horse can do. "Distance" horses are in excellent physical shape and well-conditioned long before they attempt to cover this kind of ground. It takes many months for a rider or trainer to get a horse ready to travel a 100-mile race.

Such races, by the way, are called endurance rides and are sanctioned in the United States by the American Endurance Ride Conference (AERC). The most famous endurance ride conducted in the United States is the Western States Trail Ride, more commonly known as the Tevis Cup. This challenging ride is held every year in the Sierra Nevada in northern California and features the country's top endurance horses racing for 100 miles in one day. (Other 100-mile races are held throughout the country, as well as shorter endurance rides of 50 and 25 miles.)

The breed of horse best known for success in endurance rides is the Arabian. Developed in the Middle East, the Arabian horse was bred to cover long distances in short periods of time. Bred for stamina, Arabians and part-Arabians dominate long-distance riding around the world.

HAPPY TRAILS TO ME

I loved to trail ride as a child, so when I grew up and found out about endurance riding, I became intrigued. *What must it be like to ride a horse for hours a day*, I wondered, *through scenic countryside and well-planned trails?* I vowed I would try this sport someday, somehow.

My chance to dabble in endurance came one evening at a friend's party. I was chatting with then-associate editor of *Horse Illustrated* magazine, Jennifer Nice, who happened to be an avid endurance rider. I told her my interest in trying competitive trail, a form of endurance riding that wasn't as long and was generally less intense than the 100-mile races so well-known in the horse world. (Competitive trail riding, sanctioned by the North American Trail Ride Conference, or NATRC, is not a race but a judged competition on the trail.) Jennifer told me that she had an older Arabian gelding named Oash, who was a former endurance horse, I could borrow if I wanted to give competitive trail riding a try, and that she and I could attend a ride together.

Not one to give up an opportunity to live out a dream, especially with an experienced endurance rider such as Jennifer at my side, I took her up on her offer. We scoped out upcoming competitive trail rides and found one scheduled for four months away. We began meeting several times a week to ride and condition the horses, me on Oash and Jennifer on Sam, a young Arabian she was training for a career in endurance.

The day before our competitive trail ride, we loaded up the horses in Jennifer's trailer and headed out. We camped overnight as required by NATRC rules and set out on our ride the next morning.

Oash was the perfect horse, calmly strolling down the trails as Jennifer and I took in the scenery. Because part of the ride was held on private land, we came across some interesting livestock along the way, including a herd of Watusi cattle with horns spanning six feet across and a herd of zebras with plenty of crazy stripes. Our horses stopped in their tracks at the sight of both of these unusual animals, a distinct "What the heck is THAT?" look written all over their faces.

Although parts of the trail we covered seemed remote, we were very conscious of the fact that we were being judged the entire way. Every so often, we'd come across a judge along the trail who would ask us to dismount and mount, walk our horses through water, back up, or follow some other instruction intended to illustrate our competence as riders.

Fortunately, the judges were few and far between. Most of our ride was relaxed and quiet. We rode through cool, bubbling creeks, gazed down at a turquoise lake from a ridgeline trail, and watched our horses graze in a meadow. After twenty-four miles of riding, we eventually rode into camp, tired but happy.

For Jennifer and Oash, this was just one more fun endurance ride on a long list of accomplishments. For me—who won second place in horsemanship— it was the beginning of a new passion.

Audrey Pavia

Q: **What's the relationship of horsepower in engines to the power of a horse?**

A: *"Horsepower" was a catchy term* introduced by James Watt in the eighteenth century to help people understand the potential of his steam engine. The term caught on, and most people today think of horsepower when it comes to comparing the output of internal combustion engines in our automobiles. Somewhat appropriate, when you think of it, since the internal combustion engine was most responsible for putting most horses out of a job. In most technical applications, however, the more common and accurate term used to measure power is the watt, named after James himself. One horsepower converts to about 750 watts, by the way.

So what is a one horsepower, in practical terms? One horsepower is equal to the energy it takes to lift 33,000 pounds one foot in one minute, which was what Watt guessed a horse was capable of doing after studying mine ponies. In fact, for short bursts a horse can man-age a horsepower rating of almost fifteen, but over the long haul can sustain less than a single horsepower's worth of output.

Q: How do directors get horses to fall down in movies?

A: Fortunately, we live in the age of humane treatment for movie horses—at least in the United States. American films shot over the last thirty years feature horses who have been trained to fall. Thanks to the efforts of an organization called American Humane, filmmakers make the humane treatment of movie horses a priority.

Sorry to say, it wasn't always this way. Before American Humane got involved in 1940 and started putting pressure on the movie industry, with the help of the American public, filmmakers often forced horses to do very dangerous—and often fatal—stunts. Today's falling horses are trained to drop to the ground on their sides with a cue from the rider. They land on marks (designated spots) that have been prepared with soft bedding so the horses (and riders) aren't hurt. In the old days, however, horses were regularly tripped with a device called a Running W, which caused them to flip head over heels at a full gallop.

This made for dramatic footage but often dead or injured horses.

Just as horses can be taught to fall safely for the camera, they can also be taught a variety of tricks. Roy Rogers's horse, Trigger, had a whole repertoire of gags, including a famous stunt he performed with Bob Hope in *Son of Paleface,* released in 1952. Trigger and Hope were forced to share a bed together, but Trigger would not let Hope have the covers.

Just about any horse can be taught to do tricks, although some have more talent than others. Hollywood trainers look for horses with playful personalities to be trick horses.

Trick horses have been trained to perform all sorts of antics, including drinking from a bottle, riding in the backseat of a car, carrying objects in their mouths, knocking people over with their noses, and more. Without trick horses, going to the movies would be a lot less fun.

Why do some horses have longer manes and tails than others?

A: *For the same reason that some people* have naturally red hair and others brown. It's all in the genes!

Certain breeds of horses are known for having especially long, thick manes and tails. The Andalusian, for example, is famous for flowing locks—especially the stallions. Andalusians pass their gorgeous manes and tails along to their offspring.

The Friesian is another breed known for its cascading mane and tail. Some Friesians have such long tails that they drag on the ground.

Mane and tail length varies within breeds, too. Particular bloodlines within a breed will display longer hair than others in the same breed.

Although nature is the primary reason for a long mane and tail, nurture can also play a part. Even the flimsiest mane and tail can be made to grow a bit longer with tender, loving care. Tails that are washed, braided, and kept in "tail bags" will grow faster than tails left on their own.

Manes that are washed and braided also have a chance of lengthening. Likewise, rough treatment can make even the most luxurious mane and tail ratty. Repeated combing through the hair, especially if it's dirty, can cause the hairs to break off, leaving a shorter, less glorious mane and tail.

Q: **Why the differences between English and Western riding? Not just the saddles but the clothes and even the bits and reins seem different.**

A: English and Western styles of riding are very different, and with good reason. Riding styles are called "disciplines," and these two disciplines have very distinct histories that lead to the differences we see today.

Let's start with English riding, which has a few sub-disciplines. The two most common are hunt seat and dressage. Hunt seat started in England in the 1600s and was designed for the British upper crust. Hunt seat features a small, somewhat flat saddle that positions the rider's body forward for jumping. British nobles participated in their favorite sport, foxhunting, with this saddle. Foxhunting entailed galloping through the fields of the British countryside in pursuit of the hounds (who in turn were in pursuit of the fox), leaping over hedges and fences along the way. Because this type of riding required considerable control over the horse (horses get pretty excited when they are foxhunting), two hands were used on the reins. The reins were connected directly to the bit. These days, hunt seat is still used for foxhunting, as well as in competitive equine events that call for jumping.

The other English subdiscipline, dressage, was developed in Europe from military riding. Called "horse ballet" by some, dressage requires very distinct maneuvers to be performed by the horse with only subtle cues from the rider. Dressage saddles are less flat than hunt seat saddles and allow the rider to sit more upright. Dressage riders at the upper levels (such as those who ride in the Olympics) often use bridles with two bits inside the horse's mouth and ride with both hands on two sets of reins.

Western is the most popular riding discipline in the United States. Heavily influenced by the Mexican vaqueros (cowboys) who worked cattle in the California territory in the early 1800s, Western is a working discipline.

American cowboys used modified versions of the Mexican saddle to create the Western saddle we see today, with its deep seat, heavy stirrups, and trademark horn. Because cowboys needed one hand free at all times to deal with the cattle, holding the reins with one hand became a tradition in Western riding. Cowboys, like the vaqueros before them, used "leverage bits," which allowed them to have more control over the height of the horse's head—a valuable tool when chasing cows. Leverage bits such as the curb are still in use today in Western riding.

Q: Will a panicked horse really run back into a burning barn?

A: *Yes, unfortunately.* This tendency to run toward a blazing barn is one of the many consequences of domestication for the horse. Horses who live in stalls have come to associate the barn with safety and security, instead of the great outdoors. The barn is the place where they eat, sleep, and spend most of their time. When a fire starts in a barn, people who are trying to save the horses often turn them loose to get the animals away from the burning building. The chaos that ensues causes the horses to panic, which in turn sends them running back to the place where they feel most secure: the barn.

Experts on how to handle horses during disasters recommend that rescuers close the barn door after the horses are turned loose. This will prevent them from running back into danger.

Q: Why do horses neigh so much in the movies?

A: *I don't know about you,* but that drives us crazy. Every time we're watching a movie and a horse appears on screen, a whinny is sure to follow. If you'd never spent any time around real-life horses, you'd think they all walk around neighing constantly, for absolutely no reason.

For some purpose we've yet to figure out, filmmakers seem to think they need to have whinnying sounds in the background of every scene that includes a horse. Perhaps they think it creates more drama and tension. Or maybe they think you won't notice the cowboy is riding a horse if you don't also hear the animal. Or perhaps, at this point, it's just part of moviemaking tradition, taught at film schools throughout the United States as part of Sound Effects 101: "Turn to page fifteen of your textbook and read the section on fake horse noises. There will be a quiz."

In reality, horses neigh only when there is good reason. They neigh to greet other horses and favorite humans they see in the distance. They neigh if you think you are about to give them a treat. And they neigh when they are separated from other horses and want to reconnect with their herd.

They don't neigh when they are dozing at a hitching post in front of the town saloon. They don't neigh when they are being galloped into a scene as their rider delivers an urgent message to another rider. And they sure as heck don't neigh with their mouths closed!

Q: **Do horses like to jump?**

A: *Some horses do!* They get genuinely excited when they know they are going to be asked to jump, and do so with great relish.

Whether a horse enjoys this activity depends on the horse's personality, natural talents, and how well he was trained. That's right: horses must be trained to jump. Even though a horse can do it naturally (wild horses can leap over rocks and logs if they need to), jumping with a rider on its back is a lot different from jumping solo. Also, in order to be able to scale the kinds of jumps that top show jumpers are asked to negotiate—six feet or higher—a horse has to have special training.

When jumping horses are trained, they start out with just poles on the ground that they have to trot over. Eventually they are asked to leap over a small simple jump. This is followed by a series of small jumps, and then higher, more complicated jumps. By using this gradual progression, trainers help horses build their confidence and teach them the nuances of jumping a course; that is, a series of complicated jumps.

If a horse is good at jumping and has been trained to have confidence, chances are he will enjoy this activity. It's a lot more exciting than just going around in circles in an arena!

Q: **Does a horse need to have a bit to be ridden?**

A: *Most horses are ridden with a bit,* but plenty aren't. Some are ridden with devices called hackamores, while a few are ridden only with a rope around their necks.

Bits work primarily by putting pressure on the roof of the horse's mouth, the tongue, and the "bars" of the mouth (the lower gums). Hackamores, on the other hand, primarily put pressure on the horse's nose and chin. Mechanical hackamores have leather nosebands attached to metal shanks that hang down and attach to a chain under the chin as well as to the reins. A bosal hackamore is a teardrop-shaped device made from rawhide that goes around the horse's nose. The reins attach to a loop under the horse's jaw, and control is maintained through pressure on the horse's nose.

Some highly trained horses can be ridden with nothing but a rope around their necks. These horses have learned to respond to the rider's legs, voice, and weight in a way that doesn't require a bridle. To stop such a specially trained horse, all the rider needs to do is give a gentle tug on the neck rope. And really skilled trainers can stop a horse without a rope at all—just by the subtle shift in their weight when they think *stop*!

Q: **Are horses afraid of snakes? Will they run from them, step over them, or stomp them?**

A: *In the movies, horses are afraid* of snakes. They will run from them, rear up when they see them, and sometimes deliberately stomp on them to save their favorite human or other horses from these evil reptiles.

In reality, horses don't pay much attention to snakes. They don't know to be afraid of them unless they have had a bad experience with a snake. Even horses who have been bitten by a poisonous snake may not even know they were bitten, even though they can become very ill.

Most horses simply ignore snakes. Riders, on the other hand, have a tendency to freak out when they see a snake, especially if the snake is of a venomous variety. A lot of horses are very sensitive, and if a rider becomes anxious, the horse will also get pretty nervous. A horse may not know why the rider is afraid, but the animal will guess there must be good reason to be worried.

If you are riding along on the trail and see a snake,

don't count on your horse to spook and run off or to stomp the thing to death, rescuing both of you from those treacherous fangs. Chances are, your horse won't even notice the snake at all.

Q: **Do horses prefer to live alone or with another horse?**

A: *Horses don't like living alone.* Many will tolerate it, but all prefer to be with other horses.

Like humans, horses are very social animals. In fact, in a way, horses are more social than humans, because for them, the company of their own kind is perceived as an issue of life or death. In the wild, a horse living alone is more vulnerable to predators. There is safety in numbers, and horses know it.

Horses also get very lonely without other horses around. Some experts have observed that among wild horses, young stallions driven from their family herds by older, more dominant stallions were visibly depressed and forlorn.

These solo young stallions wander aimlessly, as if life isn't worth living. Rather than go on alone, some of them join up with other outcasts to form "bachelor bands." While the goal of every stallion is to have a herd of mares to call his own, stallions would rather live with other stallions—their potential rivals—than be by themselves.

Q: How did Native Americans keep their loose herds of horses from running away?

A: *They were "horse whisperers."* Several Native American tribes kept vast herds of horses at their disposal and managed to keep these herds close to their villages without using fences or other means of confinement. They pulled this off by understanding horse behavior and by being vigilant about keeping watch on the herds. They also respected their horses and bonded with them as if they were all part of the same herd.

The keepers of these horses had good motivation to keep their charges close at hand. The equine was a valuable commodity in Native American horse cultures and was used to measure individual wealth. The members of the tribe who owned the most horses were considered the richest.

Horses were important for spiritual reasons as well. For example, the individual members of the Nez Perce tribe of Idaho developed close and special relationships with their horses. The tribe had a saying: "When you're at one with your horse, you're at peace with yourself."

Although individuals owned the horses, the animals still lived in large herds that grazed close to camp. The horses were unlikely to leave the general area, even though they weren't fenced in, because tribes were good at locating the best grazing areas and setting up camp near them. In the spring, summer, and fall, the horses had plenty of good grass to eat in the areas right around the village. In the winter, camps were established in areas with an abundance of cottonwood bark, a favorite of horses forced to forage in the snow. With good eats all around them, the horses had little desire to wander away.

To help ensure that the herd stayed close to camp, members from the tribe tended the horses, keeping a close eye on them at all times. This was not only to make sure the horses didn't stray, but also to protect them from other tribes who might steal some of the horses in the dark of night.

In the Nez Perce tribe, some people were said to have a special power with horses. They could walk a circle as big or as small as they wanted and the horses would not leave its confines.

Certain individual horses were so valuable to horse-keeping tribes that they were kept inside the owner's lodge or tied close by. Usually this honor went to specially trained buffalo horses who were cherished for their ability to successfully carry riders during buffalo hunts. These prized mounts were often the targets of horse thieves from warring tribes and needed to be closely guarded.

Horses were also taught to be ground tied with a halter of sorts. Both the halter and the ground tie were made of horsehair or rawhide rope. The horse was tied to a low shrub, teepee stake, or lodgepole. The owner of the horse would sometimes tie a loop around one front leg. More rambunctious horses were hobbled (their front feet tied together to prevent them from moving quickly) using twisted rawhide hobbles.

Q: Do horses prefer some people over others? Are horses prejudiced?

A: Some horses prefer certain people above others, while other horses couldn't care less and like (or dislike) everyone equally. Generally speaking, horses prefer people who give them goodies and treat them nicely.

Many horses have an aversion to a person who reminds them of someone who has handled them roughly and unfairly. Depending on the horse, the reaction will be to run away from this person, act nervous around him or her, or become defensive by kicking or biting or threatening to do so.

Some horses are prejudiced toward certain types of humans, but not in the way people are. A horse can't be a racist like a person can. But a horse can have an aversion to a person of a certain race or gender, based on past experience. Horses who have been mistreated by men are often fine with female riders but difficult with or afraid of male riders. A horse who has been ill-used by someone of a particular race may be hostile toward a person of that same race, especially if the person is of the same gender as the abuser.

Likewise, a horse may take a particular liking to someone who reminds him of a former rider or caretaker who once showed him a lot of love and kindness.

Q: Why do horses go lame so often?

A: Although horses are big strong creatures, they are also delicate in many ways—especially in the matter of their legs.

Take a look at a racehorse. You see a strong body weighing almost 1,000 pounds with only four spindly legs to hold up that bulk. Wild equines like Przewalski's Horse, a native of Mongolia that is the closest living animal to the prehistoric horse, have smaller bodies and thicker legs. Domestic breeding has taken a horse that once looked like Przewalski's and turned it into a much larger, longer-legged creature.

Combine this reality of anatomy with the way domestic horses are often kept—in stalls with little room or incentive to move around—and you have great potential for leg problems. In the wild, horses move around constantly as they graze, often covering as many as twenty miles in one day. In captivity, horses stand around a lot, which is not good for their legs.

Hard work and poor hoof care also contribute to lameness. Domestic horses are asked to do many things they would never do in the wild, such as rope cattle, jump over high fences, and come to sliding stops. Combine that with often improper trimming and shoeing, and you have a recipe for disaster.

All this adds up to a host of leg problems common in today's horses, such as laminitis (inflammation of the soft tissue of the hoof wall), navicular problems (physical breakdown of the hoof's navicular bone), and arthritis. It seems that lameness is the price many domestic horses pay for their food and board.

Q: **I've heard horses and goats make good friends. Is this true?**

A: *Horses are social animals* and often make friends with members of species other than their own. Goats seem to be a particularly popular companion for horses.

Horses and goats probably get along well because they are both very social herd animals. Why goats get along better with horses than, say, sheep, is up for debate, although it could be because goats are just as smart as horses, if not smarter.

That said, not all goats like horses and vice versa. In fact, the first time most horses see a goat, they do a double-take. If the horse is of the less brave variety, he might even turn and run, thinking he was seeing some kind of monster with hooves and horns. It doesn't take long for most horses to figure out that goats are basically harmless and actually make good buddies.

In addition to goats, certain breeds of dogs are more popular with horse people, giving folks the impression that these breeds are better with horses than others. It's really not true, however. Any breed of dog can be taught to get along well with horses. It's just that two breeds in particular—the Pembroke Welsh Corgi and the Jack Russell Terrier—seem to be more popular among horse owners.

Why? Who knows. It could be because the Pembroke is a small herding dog who isn't hyper and not terribly threatening to horses. And horse people just like them. Jack Russells are handy to have around the stable because they are expert rodent catchers and can do wonders at keeping rats and mice out of the horse's grain.

MILAGRO
MEETS STAR

Goats and horses are known for how well they get along. They are often seen grazing in pastures together or sleeping side-by-side in the noonday sun. But not all goats and horses get along. Remember the movie *Seabiscuit*? In one scene, the racehorse let his feelings about goats be known when he sent one of the poor creatures sailing out of his stall.

Sometimes it's not the horse who is the problem, but the goat. One day my Spanish Mustang, Milagro, went with me to my trainer's house. My trainer has three goats who roam her property at will. One of them is a stinky old buck named Star.

Star is a pygmy goat, so he is short in stature. But that doesn't keep him from walking around the place acting as if he is the lord and master.

Apparently Star has decided that all the horses on the property belong to him. So when I brought Milagro over on that day, Star took considerable notice of Milagro. This new horse did not belong to him. At least not yet.

Milagro is a brave horse and quite the character himself. A friend once described him as being "like the kid in the picture holding up his fingers behind someone's head." He's an imp and a prankster who will pull your hat off your head if you're not looking or remove tools from your back pocket and run away with them. But that day, Milagro the prankster met his match in Star the goat.

As Milagro stood quietly minding his own business (for a change) while my trainer and I stood chatting nearby, Star barged up to him and tried to press his horns against Milagro's shoulder. Milagro had seen goats before, but not one who acted like this. He turned away from Star, only to find the pushy goat following right after him, again trying to press his horns against the horse's shoulder. Milagro made another evasive maneuver, but to no avail. Pretty soon, Milagro was pivoting around and around on his hindquarters, swinging his front end away from Star as the persistent ruminant continued in hot pursuit. It was pretty funny watching the prankster being outpranked, but I reluctantly had to step in and shoo Star away before Milagro had a nervous breakdown. He was starting to get pretty freaked out.

Now, whenever Milagro sees goats, his head goes up and his ears prick forward, his eyes wide as he searches the flock. No doubt he's looking to make sure Star isn't lurking in there somewhere, waiting to get him.

Audrey Pavia

Q: Why do some people like the smell of horse manure?

A: *If you are a fanatical horse person,* chances are you love the aroma, much to the horror of your non-horsey friends.

Horse people love the smell of manure just as auto freaks love the smell of a new car, because it floods us with wonderful memories of days spent in the company of horses.

If you've never smelled horse manure, you must take a whiff someday. Made up of digested plant material, it bears no olfactory resemblance to dog or cat poo. Instead, it has a sweet, rich smell that means horses—the most glorious of creatures—are close at hand.

Q: How hard is it to adopt a wild horse? Can they be trained to be ridden?

A: *It's not hard to adopt a wild horse.* In fact, the U.S. Bureau of Land Management (BLM) encourages it!

The BLM regularly rounds up bands of wild horses from federal lands and puts them up for adoption at BLM facilities. These horses range from very young foals to older stallions. The horses are completely wild and have never been handled by humans, yet they are up for adoption to anyone who wants one, provided you have the proper facilities.

In order to qualify to adopt a wild horse, you must be eighteen years or older, be free from convictions for animal abuse or neglect, have at least a 20 x 20–foot sheltered corral with 5-foot-high fencing, and be able to cough up $125 to $200 for the adoption fee. You must also have access to a stock-style horse trailer so you can pick up the horse and bring him home.

Wild horses can most definitely be trained for riding. The riding trails and horse show arenas are full of formerly wild horses that are not only trained for riding but are excellent mounts. Wild horses are known for being hardy and having plenty of endurance, so they make especially good trail horses.

The only caveat to adopting a wild horse is that it can be a challenge to tame and train them if you are new to horses. Experienced horse trainers have no trouble making good riding horses out of adopted wild ones, though. Plus, it's pretty cool to know you are riding a horse who used to be wild.

Q: What's the difference between a mustang and a wild horse?

A: *Depends on who's being asked.* Many people use the terms "mustang" and "wild horse" interchangeably. When used this way, the terms refer to bands of feral horses that are managed by the U.S. Bureau of Land Management. Wild horse herds managed by the BLM can be found in many Western states, as well as a few in the Midwest.

In most cases, these feral horses are the descendants of domestic horses that escaped from ranchers over the past 100 or so years (some more recently). They have varied bloodlines, with everything from draft horse to pony. Periodically, the BLM rounds up bands of these feral horses and puts them up for adoption to the public.

The number of horses rounded up each year is a constant source of controversy. Ranchers and environmentalists want the numbers of feral horses brought down to very small numbers. Wild horse advocates believe the horses have the right to the public land and should be left alone. A law passed in 1971 makes it illegal for individuals to round up or harm wild horses. Before this law was passed, wild horses were frequently captured and sold for dog food. (Marilyn Monroe's last film, *The Misfits,* released in 1961, addresses this issue in its story line.)

While many people refer to feral horses as mustangs, another set of horses are also called mustangs: specifically, Spanish Mustangs. Unlike the mixed-blood horses found on the open range, Spanish Mustangs are direct descendents of the horses brought to the New World by the Spaniards in the 1500s. In the 1950s, isolated bands of these horses were found in various parts of the West and efforts were made to save them. Today, a few thousand of these horses, registered with a number of different Spanish Mustang organizations, can be found in the United States.

Because different strains of mustangs of Spanish descent are represented in this breed, other names like the Colonial Spanish Horse and Horse of the Americas are used to refer to this type of horse. These terms also help distinguish the purebred Spanish Mustang from the feral horse, sometimes called the "BLM mustang."

Q: Why do horses need their feet cleaned?

A: *In large part because of* a nasty fungus called "thrush." Thrush is an ugly, smelly infection that likes to grow on the underside of the horse's hoof. It tends to attack the grooves on either side of the frog (the frog is the triangle-shaped part of the hoof anatomy on the underside), the indentation in the frog itself, and the area around the inside edge of the hoof. Thrush loves dark, damp places with organic material to feed on. When a horse's hoof becomes packed with manure, damp bedding, and mud (something that occurs easily to stabled horses wearing shoes), thrush has a picnic feeding on the tissue of the horse's hoof. If untreated, it can spread deep into the horse's hoof.

Fortunately, thrush is easy to treat. Horse owners can buy thrush medications over the counter at feed stores to apply directly to the hoof. They won't work very well, however, unless the root of the problem—chronic wetness in the feet—is corrected, allowing the hooves to get (and stay) dry.

Another reason people clean out horses' feet is to remove rocks that can become lodged in the grooves around the frog. A trapped rock can cause the horse's sole to bruise, resulting in a lame horse.

Q: Do horses like to be in parades?

A: *That depends on the horse.* By nature, horses don't appreciate noise and chaos, two factors present in most parades. But some horses are inherently less flappable than others. Combine an easygoing personality with the right training, and you can end up with a horse who actually enjoys the stimulation that a parade provides.

A prospective parade horse must undergo a lot of training under saddle before even attending his first parade. The horse must be so well trained that he automatically responds to his rider regardless of what's going on around him. This ensures the horse behaves safely on the parade route. Next, the horse must be exposed to a variety of different environments and situations.

Some people spend time desensitizing their horses to loud noises and scary sights long before they take them to their first parade. They do this by taking the animal to horse shows just to hang out so the horse can get used to the chaos. They may also take the horse on a group trail ride to get him used to being around a lot of other horses in an exciting situation (most horses find trail riding with a bunch of other horses very stimulating). Some prospective parade horse owners sign their equines up for formal "de-spooking" clinics that expose the horse to all kinds of sights and sounds.

Other people simply start the training process by entering their horses in small parades to get the horses used to this environment. Local parades are the best choice since the chaos at these community events is not as great as that in a large parade. Community parades are also best because they feature the least amount of spectators. This means fewer people to be embarrassed in front of if your horse freaks out and dumps you.

By the time any horse gets to the point where he can be part of a big event like the Rose Parade, he has participated in a number of smaller parades. This is a requirement of most large-parade committees, who want to make sure they don't show an audience of millions the antics of a terrified horse.

Q: Why do some horses foam at the mouth when being ridden?

A: **When it comes to horses,** foaming at the mouth is a good thing. In fact, it's the sign of a happy, healthy horse, not a rabid animal as some might think.

Nine times out of ten, when you see foam on a horse's lips, it's because the horse is wearing a bit in his mouth. His saliva glands will produce moisture in response to the bit resting on the lower gums of his mouth. When a horse is relaxed and carrying his head in the proper way to respond to the rider's cues through the reins, his saliva glands flow freely. On the other hand, horses that are tense and not carrying their heads in the right position when being ridden will have a dry mouth.

Next time you see a horse on TV, in a parade, or just walking down the trail with foam around his mouth, take comfort in knowing he's doing exactly what he's supposed to do.

Q: **How does "getting a leg up on the competition" relate to horses?**

A: *"To get a leg up"* means getting an advantage or boost. Some people may think booster seat, but in this case it's booster foot. In the horse world, it's when a rider is helped—actually lifted—by another rider's hands when mounting a horse. Getting a boost in this context is more like getting a lift.

The helper creates a "hand" stirrup by lacing together the fingers on both hands for extra support. The rider being assisted sticks one shin into the cupped hands. The rider then gets a lift up into the saddle. The gesture is also a racetrack way of saying, "Good luck!" (And much better in such circumstances than the traditional theater world wish of "Break a leg!")

Q: Do they really send old horses to the glue factory?

A: *Not anymore. In the old days,* horses who could no longer work were shipped off to be slaughtered, and their bones and hooves made into glue. It was a sad and tragic way for a horse who had worked so hard in the service of humans to come to the end of his life.

These days, natural glues are made from the bones and hooves of cattle who have been slaughtered for food. (Ever wondered about that cow on the front of the Elmer's Glue bottle?) Synthetic glues are also readily available, and don't contain any animal products.

"Useless" horses are not off the hook, however. These days, instead of going to the glue factory, many unwanted horses end up being slaughtered for food. Horse slaughter facilities in the United States ship horsemeat to France and Japan, where it is considered a delicacy.

Many horse lovers consider this practice a travesty and are fighting to make it illegal to sell horses for slaughter. At press time, Congress is considering a bill that would outlaw horse slaughter in the United States.

Q: How can you guess a horse's age by looking at his teeth?

A: *Horses are grazing animals.* Because they eat mostly roughage, the most efficient way to get nutrition is to grind the food into small particles. Their teeth are well designed for grinding. But because teeth are not made of metal, as they grind, they wear. By nature horses eat a lot and grind a lot, and if their teeth didn't continue to grow, they'd run out of teeth eventually. This growth, combined with the natural receding of the gum line and other factors, helps veterinarians and other experts to guess a horse's age pretty reliably.

The length of the teeth is not the only factor. The way the teeth wear is another way to judge the age of a horse. By looking at the centers of the teeth, you can see various marks in the pulp that indicate the amount of wear the tooth has experienced.

Something called the "Galvayne's groove," a vertical line in the tooth, is found on the upper corner incisor and can also be a good indicator of a horse's age. The groove usually appears when a horse reaches ten years of age. By the time the horse is fifteen, the groove has gone halfway down the tooth. At the age of twenty, the line is almost completely to the bottom. By age twenty-five, the line has started to disappear and only appears on half of the tooth. When the horse hits the age of thirty, the Galvayne's groove is gone.

Eventually the teeth do stop growing. Geriatric horses start losing what little is left of their teeth around twenty-five to twenty-seven years of age.

The development and growth of teeth in a horse is very systematic and consistent. If a horse has normal dentition and good conformation of the jaw, experts can very reliably estimate a horse's age by his teeth. Even so, each horse wears his teeth differently, different feeds will affect tooth wear differently, and not all horses of the same age have exactly the same look to their teeth.

The teeth of domestic horses wear unevenly when they eat, leaving sharp points on uneven surfaces. These points can cause pain or even sores when the horse chews or when a bit is placed in the mouth. When this happens, the horse needs a veterinarian to come out with a file and work on his teeth, a procedure called "floating."

Q: How well do horses hear and smell?

A: *Horses hear and smell pretty well*—much better than humans do. They need to if they want to get a jump on predators who might be lurking behind bushes and around blind corners. If you can hear or smell the mountain lion before you can see it, you'll have a head start!

Let's look at the horse's hearing first. The equine ear is shaped somewhat like a funnel. Using a set of muscles to swivel in a few different directions, the horse's ear catches sound waves like a satellite dish receiver and channels the sound down into the ear canal, where it is detected and transmitted to the brain. One study showed that horses can hear sounds as far away as 4,400 meters (or approximately 2.75 miles). They are also able to hear higher-pitched sounds than we can.

When it comes to smell, horses rely heavily on their ability to detect scents. They can pick up the most subtle of odors with their large, flaring nostrils. They catch scents on the wind and will often react to them. If a horse catches a scent belonging to an unfamiliar animal, he will often become tense and wary. For instance, a horse who has never seen or smelled cattle can become rather alarmed at first until he figures out that these animals are harmless.

Horses use scent to identify each other, too, and not just by sniffing nose to nose. A lot of horses will stop to sniff piles of manure left on the trail, most likely to get an idea of who it was who left behind this smelly calling card. Foals recognize their mothers largely by smell, too. Experiments where the nostrils of foals were coated with mentholated ointment to prevent them from smelling anything else left these babies unable to discern which mare in the herd was Mom.

Q: **What is the largest load a horse can carry?**

A: *The question should be what is* the largest load a horse can *safely* carry. Most horses will carry as much weight as you foist onto them, but whether they *should* carry a very heavy load is another question.

The general rule of thumb is that horses should not be asked to carry more than 20 percent of their body weight. Since 1,000 to 1,200 pounds is the average weight for a horse, anyone weighing more than 200 pounds is pushing it considering the saddle adds weight too. (Some Western saddles weigh as much as 35 pounds.) Heavy riders should ride larger horses who can more safely accommodate the extra weight. Also, riders who are in the upper weight limits for a horse and are not experienced riders pose an even greater burden since they are not skilled at knowing how to balance.

What happens to a horse when it carries more than it should? Back problems are likely, as well as leg problems if a horse is repeatedly asked to carry too much weight while working hard.

Q: Do horseshoes really bring good luck?

A: Some people swear that horseshoes bring good luck; others say it's just a silly superstition.

The idea of horseshoes as good luck charms started centuries ago, probably with the Celts. They believed that iron repelled fairies, mischievous supernatural creatures who were always pestering humans and making life more difficult. If you hung an iron horseshoe on your door—and horseshoes were very easy to come by in those days—you might just keep fairies from bothering your household. Some historians think the Romans may have adopted this tradition, making the habit of hanging horseshoes for good luck a widespread practice that persists to this day.

How to hang the horseshoe is a topic of debate. Some traditions dictate that you hang the horseshoe so that the ends are facing upward so the shoe can hold good luck inside. Other cultures believe that if you hang the shoe with the points downward, the luck would pour into your home.

The way you obtained the horseshoe is also important. In order for the shoe to bring you good luck, you must have found the shoe, not purchased it or stolen it. Also, the owner of the horseshoe is the one who gets the good luck from it, not the person who hangs it up.

Q: **How much water can a horse drink?**

A: *The old adage is true.* You can lead a horse to water, but you can't make him drink. Really. But you *can* encourage him, by making sure the available water is clean, fresh, free of slobber, and a nice, comfortably cool (but not too cold) temperature. If that's not enough to tempt him to drink, a teaspoon of Karo syrup squirted into his mouth often does the trick.

The old saying comes from the fact that travelers on horseback often didn't know when they would come across their next water source. While they knew no water lay ahead for miles, their horses didn't. So if the rider came across some water, led his horse to it, and tried to get the animal to drink up while he had the chance, he would discover the truth in the old adage. You can lead a horse to water, but if he's not thirsty, he's not going to drink no matter how much you beg.

Why was it so important to get the horse to drink anyway? Because water is vital to the equine digestive system. Without adequate amounts of water, horses can't digest and pass the roughage they eat. They also suffer dramatically from dehydration when working hard in the heat. Without water, horses die quickly.

Horses drink from ten to thirty gallons of water a day, depending on how hard they work, what they are eating, and the temperature of the air and the water.

Q: Can horses swim?

A: *Horses, like most other* four-legged creatures, are born knowing how to swim. For some reason, swimming is in their genes. Unlike humans, they instinctively know what to do when they hit the water. While some horses do sink at first until they figure out what to do, they don't have to be actually shown how to move in the water. This part comes naturally.

When a horse swims, he uses what would be a trotting or pacing motion on land. With his head above the water, he paddles using his legs and hooves.

Because horses have to labor to breathe when they are swimming, they can't do it for too long before becoming exhausted if they aren't used to it. When horses have been studied swimming in training pools (a method of cross-training sometimes used for racehorses), they have been able to swim about four to five minutes without a problem. By slowly building up this time, a horse can eventually swim for up to an hour.

Q: What does it mean when a horse "cribs"?

A: *Cribbing, a bad word in the equine* vernacular, is the term for a destructive and addictive behavior present in a small percentage of the horse population.

When a horse cribs, he grasps on to a horizontal object with his top front teeth, tightens his neck muscles, and sucks in air with a grunt. Horses who crib usually partake of this habit while in their stalls, although some horses will do it anywhere.

Horse owners hate cribbing. Not only is it destructive to the horse's stall (especially wood stalls, which are quickly worn down by the cribber's grasping teeth), but it is also destructive to the horse. Cribbing can wear the horse's front teeth down to nubs. Some people also believe it can cause certain muscles in the horse's neck to become overdeveloped.

Horses have been cribbing since humankind began confining them to stalls hundreds of years ago, but only recently has any serious research been conducted on this problem. Researchers are currently investigating the link between equine digestive issues and cribbing. So far, studies have determined that a high-carbohydrate diet can lead a horse to develop the habit of cribbing. Researchers also believe the behavior may be related to pain from acidic levels in the digestive system. Still others believe it's a form of neurotic behavior, a side effect of being locked up in a stall for days on end.

The tendency to crib seems to have a genetic component as well. Certain bloodlines seem to carry the propensity of cribbing. If a young horse is deprived of roughage and is confined to a small area, his genes may prompt him to start cribbing.

Q: **What's the difference between nickering, whinnying, and neighing?**

A: Although horses use body language as their primary way of communicating, they also have a varied vocal repertoire.

The differences between the nicker, the whinny, and the neigh are subtle, but people who spend a lot of time around horses can tell the difference.

The nicker is a soft chortle of sorts, usually reserved for special people or other horses. Mother horses often nicker to their foals as a way of greeting or reassuring them at close range and expressing happiness at their presence. Horses nicker at people for the same reason.

The whinny is much louder than the nicker, and fairly high-pitched. It's a greeting for horses or special people, and has an edge of excitement to it.

The neigh is very similar to the nicker, although it tends to be a bit deeper and louder, and is often uttered in anxiety. Horses separated from their herdmates, or who are otherwise uptight and want to communicate their emotions to other horses, will let out a loud neigh. Watch out if you are standing right next to a neighing horse. It's deafening!

What Is Your Horse Trying to Tell You?

Researchers are analyzing horse vocalizations to determine how stress is communicated when horses whinny. They've determined that the horse's whinny consists of two elements: a constant tone with varied harmonics that increase as the horse becomes more agitated and a variation in frequency that may be associated with communication or expression. Put another way, when the old gray mare calls her partner a "horse's ass," he knows she's stressing-out by the sound of her voice. Sound familiar?

Scientists have found that all equine vocalizations, including those of donkeys and zebras, have complex spectrums, wide bandwidths, and varying frequency. And while a donkey's bray is acoustically rich—like the tuba in the high school band—these animals have little control over the content of their sounds. Still, all equine sounds are much more complex than those of most domestic animals. Under high-stress conditions, a horse's neigh can sound like a high-pitched scream, but in calm conditions, especially when a horse's vision is restricted, scientists say that the whinnies have a rich and variable sound.

Q: **Are horses ticklish?**

A: *Although they are big and strong,* horses have some very sensitive parts on their bodies. One of the most sensitive spots is the flanks, the area between the thigh and the belly. Touch a horse's flanks with a spur and you might get a big buck in response.

The belly is the most ticklish area on the horse. A lot of horses—especially mares, it seems—will pin their ears and swish their tails in protest when you reach underneath them to brush their bellies. It's ticklish and sensitive down there, and with good reason. This is one of the most vulnerable places on a horse's body. A predator can quickly kill a horse if the animal tears at the horse's belly with fangs or claws.

Horses also have plenty of "itchy" spots that will elicit some funny faces when scratched. The chest just below the neck is one, or on the side of the withers. Give a horse a good scratching in one of these places and you'll see him extend his neck and twist his upper lip around as if to say, "Ahhh, that feels good!"

Q: What's the difference between hot-blooded, warm-blooded, and cold-blooded horses?

A: *Most horses in Old Europe* were closely related strains of calm horses used primarily to pull wagons or plows. Careful foot placement and the ability to ignore anything out of the ordinary made the calmness of these horses a virtue. They were also superb warhorses, able to ignore the chaos of the battlefield while carrying armored warriors on their backs for hours. These massive steeds were the tanks of their day, trampling all before them. These horses, typified today by the massive draft horse breeds, are the quintessential cold-blooded horses.

An expansion of exploration and trade eventually brought a new horse to Europe, an animal who was smaller, more agile, faster, and far more excitable than those staid draft horses. Probably related to the small warhorses of the Asian steppes, these newcomers were typified by the Arabian and the Turk horses. Athletic and spirited, the hotbloods became the darlings of the

European aristocracy, as they had already claimed the hearts of the ruling classes in their native lands. Free spirits, the hotbloods were better suited to riding than pulling anything, since their fire could be better tamed by a rider than a plowman with only long reins at his disposal.

You might think warmbloods are somewhere in the middle, but actually their behavior can be pretty "hot" because these are horses that were bred specifically to be performance animals, like what you see at Olympic trials. To have the "edge" necessary to be a winner in high-level events, you need a certain amount of 'tude, which makes a lot of warmbloods a bit challenging to deal with, especially if you're a vet and have to do things to them they don't necessarily enjoy.

Warmbloods were developed for dressage and show jumping, sports that developed from the stylized maneuvers of the European cavalries and cross-country pursuits of the upper-class hunters. For these sports, a horse needed to be calm and focused yet agile, showy, and fast.

Today you'll find the hot-blooded horses at the Thoroughbred racetrack and at any Arabian horse show. The cold-bloods can be seen at draft horse events, where the Clydesdale, Percheron, Belgian, and Shire show off their strength. Take in any dressage or show-jumping event, and you'll likely see warm-blooded breeds, such as the Hanoverian, Oldenburg, and Trakehner.

Actual "blood" doesn't set these horses apart from one another, however, since blood is blood, pretty much the same in all kinds of horses. Metabolism and muscle fibers are where you'll find the differences, with hot-blooded horses having predominately fast-twitch muscle fibers and cold-blooded horses having mostly slow-twitch muscle fibers.

The more fast-twitch muscle fibers, the greater performance over shorter periods of time and distance—perfect for a racehorse. The more slow-twitch fibers, the better for strength and endurance over time—perfect for a draft or plow horse. In the middle, the mix of slow- and fast-twitch muscle fibers gives you a horse who's well suited to sports that require short-term athleticism and endurance, such as show jumping and dressage.

Q: **How can you get an animal as large as a horse to cooperate when they don't want to, such as when the veterinarian is working on them?**

A: *Horses are big animals,* and they are sometimes uncooperative when asked to stand still for something they would rather avoid. Since they haven't yet figured out how to put a horse in a straitjacket, the next best thing is something called a twitch.

A twitch is a device that attaches to the horse's upper lip and pinches it. Twitches usually have wooden handles and a chain or metal grippers on the end. The chain or grippers attach to the tip of the horse's nose while a person holds the twitch by its handle.

Studies have shown that twitches work to subdue horses by distracting them when first applied. The horse is so busy wondering what is hanging off his nose that he forgets about whatever was upsetting him. Within a few minutes, the twitch causes the horse's brain to release endorphins, which work to relax the horse and ease any pain that may result from the veterinary procedure that is being performed (such as blood being drawn or a minor wound being stitched up). When a twitch is properly applied, the horse's head will hang down almost as if he were sedated. Once the twitch is removed, the horse returns to normal.

Some debate exists over whether or not twitches hurt the horse before the endorphins kick in. Based on the way most horses react when they first see the twitch, it's a safe guess to say the initial sensation isn't very pleasant.

Q: Do horses prefer to graze or have fast-food delivered to their stalls?

A: *While the idea of having fast-food* brought right to your stall might seem to be a preferable way to have your meals delivered (sort of the equine version of room service), horses actually like grazing much better. To understand why, you have to know the equine digestive system.

Horses evolved over the millennium to eat large quantities of grasses with little nutritional value. To get enough calories and nutrition, horses had to be able to consume a lot of this plant material. That meant grazing for hours, taking in as much of the grass as possible. The horse's digestive system evolved to accommodate this method of eating by slowly processing this fibrous plant material through approximately 100 feet of intestines. In essence, the horse's gut began to work around the clock, constantly digesting the food as the horse was eating.

Fast-forward to present day when horses are kept in stalls or paddocks without access to constant grazing, and you have animals whose minds and bodies are often in distress. Horses acquire behavioral problems because they are bored and frustrated, and they develop digestive disorders because their stomachs are often empty when they should be full.

The horse has a powerful instinct to graze and is happiest when he's doing what he evolved to do: eat grass to his heart's content.

To Graze
or Not to Graze

When a grazing cow chomps down on a tuft of grass, she thrusts her head away from herself to cut it free. That's partly because cows have no upper front teeth. But a grazing horse, who has uppers and lowers in the front, jerks his head toward himself to slice off a mouthful.

Q: Can horses smell fear?

A: *According to some experts,* horses can't smell fear, but they can sense it. Because they are prey animals living in herds, they are tuned in to the emotions of those around them. If a herdmate is fearful, the horse will pick up on this by seeing the body language of the other horse. If someone in the herd is scared, danger may be lurking. So it's imperative that horses know how to read fear.

Horses who live with humans sometimes get good at sensing human fear as well. A horse lacking in confidence mounted by a fearful rider is a recipe for trouble. The horse will sense the rider's fearfulness (through body language and by sensing the rider's tension) and think there must be something to be afraid of. The horse gets scared, which makes the rider more scared, and it becomes a vicious cycle.

Some horses are brave and confident yet are also opportunists. They sense a rider's fear and realize that the person is lacking in confidence. If the person has no confidence, then the pushy horse takes over as leader. The results are often not too good in this situation since the horse's idea of how things should go rarely coincides with the wishes of the rider.

Another theory abounds that horses can indeed smell fear. The thinking goes like this: Every animal (including humans) secretes chemicals called pheromones all the time through the skin and other bodily secretions. These pheromones change in amount and type according to season, reproductive cycles, physical activity, and stresses. We are all able to detect these pheromones, although some animals are better at this than others.

Do horses make an intellectual evaluation of these pheromones and make rational decisions based on the data? In other words, does the horse think to himself, "Hmmm, I can smell that Jane Doe over there seems a little stressed-out today, maybe a little fearful. Should I trot over there and nuzzle a carrot from her pocket? Kick her really hard? Run away with a wild-eyed look?"

Unlikely. Rather than rationally thinking it through, horses sense the pheromones. A nervous system change occurs that prepares the horse for the next action, which in a horse is typically "run away with a wild-eyed look." Since horses are herd animals and are tuned in to the fear responses of their herdmates, this is the most likely choice.

Q: Why do horses groom each other?

A: *Watching two horses* scratching each other's backs is a sweet experience, especially when you realize it's all part of the equine bonding experience.

Horses are the socialites of the animal world, and they depend heavily on each other for companionship and security. In the wild, they live in herd situations, where they bond strongly with their fellow equines.

Combine this love for one another with an obvious inability to reach certain places on the body (no hands like humans to scratch where it itches), and you have an arrangement where friendly horses gladly assist each other in removing the tickle. It's not really grooming per se since they aren't doing it to clean one another. Instead, the ritual is being performed to scratch hard-to-reach places while, at the same time, solidifying their bond.

Q: Why do horses roll after they work out or are bathed?

A: *Because it feels good!* They also roll just for the heck of it, especially when presented with nice, soft dirt or sand to thrash around in.

A few theories exist on why horses like to roll so much. One is that it's a good way to scratch an itch (backscratchers for horses haven't been invented yet). Having a saddle on your back or water dripping off you can make a horse itchy, so why not get down and rub that itch right out?

Another theory is that coating the hair with dust helps keep flies and other biting insects to a minimum. When a horse is covered with dirt or mud, it's a lot harder for a bug to find the skin below.

Some say that rolling is the horse's way of giving himself a chiropractic adjustment. All that squirming around on his back resets his vertebrae, putting everything back in order the way it's supposed to be.

Of course, if you watch a horse, you can also figure out that rolling is plain fun. A lot of horses get up after a good roll and take off running with a good buck. They are clearly saying "whoopee, that was great!" in horse language.

Q: Does it hurt when you pull on a horse's mane?

A: *Horses don't have pain sensors* at the roots of their mane hair like humans do. When you pull on a horse's mane, it's not the same as pulling on a person's hair. Most horses pay no attention to it. Because of this, riders beginning to learn how to jump are often instructed to hold the mane to help get them into proper position over fences.

That said, not all horses are forgiving about a procedure called "mane pulling," which is performed on show horses to keep their manes looking neat and tidy. Instead of cutting the mane with scissors, which leaves it blunt and unattractive, people pull hairs out of the horse's mane to thin it out for a more natural look.

Some horses don't mind the mane-pulling procedure at all and fall asleep while it's being done. Other horses will give the person doing the pulling quite a hard time, acting as if they're being tortured. It seems that in the case of those melodramatic equines, they aren't feeling actual pain, but simply don't like the sensation of having their hair pulled.

Q: How can you tell if a horse is happy?

A: *Horses don't wag their tails* like dogs or purr like cats when they want to express their happiness. They do some other things that are easily recognizable as signs of joy even to the most casual observer.

One of those signs of happiness is running and bucking. Horses will run just for the joy of it, galloping over a field with their equine friends, bucking in sheer delight. This is different from running in fear, of course. A horse who is running because he is happy has a whole different demeanor than one who is scared for his life.

Another sign of a happy horse is far more subtle. Because horses are prey animals and often on guard for their lives (we haven't been able to convince them yet that they don't need to be so vigilant now that they live in captivity), a relaxed horse is a happy horse. Not to be confused with bored or depressed, "relaxed" is usually seen when a horse is with his buddies, hanging out in a pasture, grazing on good grass or just lounging in the shade swishing at flies.

Other happy horses like to take sunbaths. On warm days, usually in the wintertime, you can sometimes see horses lying in the sun in their pastures or paddocks, all stretched out with their eyes closed. While people sometimes get scared when they see this, thinking maybe the horse is sick or dead (even the most experienced horse people have these moments of panic), it becomes obvious very quickly on closer examination that the horse is just enjoying a moment of life.

DADDY ALWAYS SAID
"YES" TO HORSES

From the time I was a little girl, and up to the time of his death, my dad called me Baby Teresa. Most everyone said he spoiled me, and I could only nod my head or smile in agreement.

When I was just three years old, I got my first horse: a beautiful palomino rocking horse. I loved my plastic palomino, but soon that wasn't good enough. I didn't want to be limited by earthly bounds: I wanted a swinging horse that was suspended in the air.

My daddy agreed.

My next horse was the real deal, a certified hay-munching, apple-eating Arabian cross. I was ten and Sandarrow was four. I wanted him the moment I laid eyes on him.

My daddy agreed.

This was the early sixties, before helmets, protective clothing, safe rider training, and the other precautions we riders take for granted today.

Sandarrow preferred to go bareback—that is, with no rider. As such, he would often rub me off on fences, run under low-hanging branches, buck like a bronco, or run full tilt back to the barn.

One day I decided to have a quick ride before a dance recital, so I jumped on Sandarrow bare-footed and bareback. He ran down the hill by our house, weaving through the trees like an equine bobsled, toward the garden where my daddy was working. I don't think I touched his back the whole way down the hill.

When we got to the garden fence, Sandarrow started bucking. I could see my dad's eyes bulging with fear as I bounced up and down off the full length of his back like a trampoline. Finally, Sandarrow spun and off I flew, hitting the ground flat on my back.

With the wind knocked out of me and dazed with a concussion, I couldn't move from where I landed, under his feet. Sandarrow stomped on my right foot, breaking nearly every bone. Then, my daddy said, he kicked with both feet, narrowly missing my head.

My daddy scooped me up in his arms and ran with me back to our house. A small man, he wasn't much larger than I was. But I remember to this day how strong he felt, how fast he moved, and how he kept looking down into my tear-filled eyes, reassuring me, "You'll be okay, Baby Teresa; Daddy has you." He wanted to get rid of Sandarrow, but I begged to keep him.

My daddy agreed.

My dad was always active, and he enjoyed robust health until he was eighty-one. That year, Mother Nature started pulling him down. He only lived a month after he was diagnosed with cancer. But during that time, we pulled out old photo albums and looked at pictures of the rocking horse and Sandarrow.

After my father died, I went into his room alone, to marinate in the essence of this diminutive man who was a giant to me. I smelled his Levis and fingered the suspenders that were still attached. I held his watch and glasses that were on the dresser. Inside the dresser, I found a cloth bag containing all of my baby teeth. Apparently, the tooth fairy and my daddy were good friends.

Finally, I sat on the edge of the same bed he'd slept in for more than sixty of his eighty years and looked at his nightstand, and at a worn diorama about the size of a deck of cards.

It was the Minnie Mouse diorama he'd bought me at Disneyland when I was six, and it featured Minnie riding a horse into the sunset. He'd customized it by putting a lock of my hair on Minnie's head and a picture of me in the painted sky behind her. My mother later told me that for more than forty years, this horse sat by my father's head, and every night my father would pat the top and say, "Good night, Baby Teresa."

I cried, asking God to take good care of this man who never said no to a girl who wanted a horse.

I know He agreed.

Teresa Becker

Q: **Why do some horses have to run in circles on a line before being ridden?**

A: Running in circles on a line is called longeing. When a horse is longed, the handler stands in the middle of a circle that the horse makes as he moves around the person at the end of a longeline, a twenty- to thirty-foot rope attached to the horse's halter or bridle.

Although longeing may look boring for the horse, it is actually a form of training. It may not seem like it, but the horse is learning as he's moving in that circle.

Many horses who have been taught how to longe have been trained with voice commands. They are taught to walk, trot, and canter on command. The handler holds a longe whip in the hand that is not holding the rope in order to cue the horse to move forward. (Most horses need only to see the whip to respond to it. Some just need to hear an occasional crack. The whip is not used to hit the horse.)

Not only does longeing help to educate the horse on how to respond to voice commands and respect the handler's cues, it also enables the horse to "get out the bugs" before being ridden. Some horses, especially young ones, have excess energy they need to release safely before a rider climbs on their back. Longeing is a good way to get the horse to exert some of that energy while also being reminded of his need to respect the wishes of his human handlers.

Q: **One swish of a tail is for flies, one's in aggravation, another is a smile of sorts. How can you tell the difference?**

A: The only way to tell the meaning behind the swish of a horse's tail is to look at the rest of his body language at the same time. If a horse is standing relaxed and quiet, half asleep in the noonday sun and you see his tail swish, he's more than likely trying to remove a fly from his legs or rump.

If you see a horse swishing his tail while pinning his ears back and baring his teeth, you know the swishes are a sign of anger.

When a baby horse swishes her tail as she trots to her mother, you can bet the swishing is a part of a happy greeting.

If you see a horse swishing his tail while being ridden, he's expressing his opinion about what the rider is asking him to do. In this case, tail swishing is considered a sign of discomfort or protest. In a sport such as dressage, tail swishing may get you marked down, because it means your horse isn't quite as happy about his work as he should be.

Q: Do spurs hurt a horse?

A: A spur, like a bit, is a signaling device used to communicate to the horse. In a car you use the gas pedal to go; in a horse you use spurs. You turn the wheel to change directions or push on the brakes to stop while driving; you use the reins connected to the bit to change directions or stop the horse.

If used violently, of course, these devices can cause pain. It's the difference between a pat on the cheek and an uppercut to the jaw. In the equine version of "different strokes for different folks," there are different kinds of spurs, only one of which is most appropriate for a particular horse doing a specific task.

Some spurs are sharp, some are dull, and others just apply pressure to the horse's sides, like jabbing someone in the ribs with your finger to get their attention. Spurs come in different shapes and lengths and are chosen based on the riding discipline and what a particular horse needs in terms of prodding.

Western spurs have round devices at the end of the spur shank called a rowel. Some rowels are big and have lots of points, while others are round and smooth. Western riders sometimes choose their spurs based on what the spur looks like—many are finely tooled and decorated—while others have them only for practical purposes and don't care much about the spur's appearance.

English riders wear spurs that look very different from the spurs of Western riders. English spurs have a relatively short neck and a blunt "prick" (the tip of the spur that comes into contact with the horse). Some English spurs are an inch or longer on the neck, while others are just stubs.

These tools, used skillfully, respectfully enhance the signals given by a skilled rider to the horse with the legs.

Q: **How do you know what kind of bit to use in a horse? What is the difference between a hard-mouthed and soft-mouthed horse?**

A: *Which bit to use on a horse is* an age-old question. You can ask two different horse trainers this question about the same horse, and you'll get two different answers.

Generally speaking, for any horse, you should use the mildest bit that will do the job—that is, get the horse to turn, stop, and hold himself together under the weight of a rider. Some horses are very sensitive and require only the mildest of bits. Other horses need more persuading, and so call for a bit that applies more pressure to their mouths.

"Hard-mouthed" and "soft-mouthed" are really misnomers because these terms imply that it's the horse's mouth that determines how well he will respond to the bit. In reality, hard-mouthed horses are those who have lost sensitivity to the bit and do not respond to it. Soft-mouthed horses, on the other hand, are very responsive to the bit and need little pressure.

It's the horse's training and attitude, not his mouth, that determines whether he is responsive to the bit. Horses who are hard-mouthed have simply learned to ignore the bit. They feel it, but they steel themselves against its pressure. Soft-mouthed horses are those who have been trained well to listen to the bit and pay attention to the message that comes through it from the rider's hands.

In certain situations, such as with police horses in a crowd, or in certain riding disciplines, such as upper-level dressage, two bits are used at the same time. This provides the rider with more control.

Q: Why did people start riding sidesaddle? Why do some do it now?

A: The concept of riding sidesaddle began in medieval times, during the era of chivalry when gallant knights rode in tournaments, battling rivals on horseback to impress their ladies. Since these tournaments often took place far from the local castle, women had to get on horseback themselves so they could follow along and witness these manly demonstrations.

But women of the Middle Ages had a dilemma. It was considered very unladylike to sit astride a horse with one leg on either side of the saddle. Plus, it was impractical given the elaborate dress women wore back then. To remedy this situation, the idea of women riding with both legs on one side of the saddle was conceived.

When they were first created, sidesaddles—which required the female rider to sit straight in the saddle with her left leg hanging straight and her right leg bent and crooked over to the left side—did not have stirrups.

Instead, women had only platforms for their left foot to rest upon and only one pommel (the rise that appears on the front of both sides of a regular saddle). Consequently, these saddles were not very safe for hard riding.

Then, in 1580, Catherine de' Medici, an enthusiastic rider (who also happened to be the queen of France), invented a sidesaddle that featured a second pommel. This second pommel allowed the lady rider to wedge her knee between the two pommels for more security in the saddle.

By the 1800s, all the well-to-do women of Europe rode sidesaddle. Another piece of equipment, the leaping pommel, was added in 1830, allowing more security for the rider. Soon women were jumping in the sidesaddle and galloping across open fields.

Today sidesaddles are made in all the same styles as traditional astride saddles, including hunt seat, saddle seat, dressage, and Western. Each of these saddles is used in its respective discipline, just as if it were an astride saddle. In fact, nearly every discipline being ridden today can also be ridden in a sidesaddle.

People who love tradition keep sidesaddle alive. Women all around the United States ride and compete in sidesaddle events to celebrate and preserve this very old style of riding.

Q: Why do horses get a swayback when they get old?

A: When a horse ages, the muscles that hold up the abdomen begin to weaken. The horse's belly begins to sag, taking the topline of the back with it. The withers stay in place and protrude upward, as do the hips. The result is a back shaped like a giant "U."

Swaybacked horses can still be ridden, depending on how bad the sway is. If it's a mild sway, it's not a problem. But a horse whose belly is hanging down to his knees is best left alone, to live out his years in a pasture somewhere with a few buddies.

What is a gait? How many kinds of gaits are there?

A: *The term "gait" refers to how* the horse moves his legs. Most horses have four gaits: walk, trot, canter, and gallop. At each of these gaits, the horse moves his legs in a different way, which creates different speeds and rhythms.

The walk is the slowest gait and has a speed of about 4 miles per hour. When a horse walks, his legs move in this order: left rear, left front, right rear, right front. Three of the horse's legs touch the ground at the same time. This creates a four-beat rhythm.

The trot is the bounciest gait. Horses tend to trot at about 9 miles per hour. The front foot and the opposite hind foot come down at the same time, making a two-beat rhythm.

The canter is the second-fastest gait, next to a gallop. In the canter, which can be anywhere from 10 miles per hour to 15, the horse extends his forelegs while also gathering the hind legs beneath the body. The legs move rhythmically with each other in the same general direction. In one phase of the canter, all four hooves come off the ground at the same time.

The gallop is probably the most famous equine gait, the one you see most in the movies. In this gait, which is similar to the canter, the horse extends his front legs at the same time he gathers his hind legs beneath him, in a four-beat rhythm. Horses can reach speeds of 40 miles per hour at this gait, although most horses gallop at 25 to 30 miles per hour.

Although most horses possess only these four gaits, some breeds—called gaited breeds, just to make things confusing—have additional gaits that have been bred into them over the centuries. Breeds like the Tennessee Walking Horse, Missouri Fox Trotter, Peruvian Paso, and Paso Fino each have their own special gait that is not a walk, trot, canter, or gallop. These special gaits, though they vary slightly between breeds, possess four-beat rhythms designed for good ground coverage and very smooth riding.

Standardbred horses have the ability to pace, which is kind of like trotting, only the front and back legs on one side move together instead of the diagonals pairing up.

Q: Why do horses wear blinkers?

A: *Horses would very much rather see* what's around them, and that's why blinkers or blinders are put on them—so they can't. Blinkers block a horse's peripheral vision, keeping them focused on their job and preventing them from being distracted. On racehorses, blinkers can range from the slightest blocking of vision—these barely there blinkers are called "cheaters"—to plastic cups so big that a horse can barely see anything alongside, even another horse.

Since a competitive nature is part of the racehorse's genetic makeup, it's not uncommon for a jockey to pull a horse's head to one side in the final stages of a race so that the animal can see that another horse is coming up beside him. Seeing another horse drawing close often prompts the animal to dig deep for something extra, all the way to the finish line.

Q: **Is it true that a horse's hoof is really his middle finger (or toe)? Where did the other toes go?**

A: *Like ballerinas in a way,* a horse is always up on his toes, except that on each of his feet, it's just the middle toe, or what it has turned into—the hoof.

The middle toe of the back foot and the middle finger of the front limb has grown and adapted to bear the entire weight of horses, and the toenails and fingernails have changed to become hooves. The heels and wrists have elevated and become the hock and front knees of the horse.

Why did this happen? Back when our ancestors were swinging from the trees, the ancestors of the horse were small animals called "eohippus." They had four toes on the front and three toes on the back leg, all with nails or tiny hooflets.

The ancient horse lived more and more on dry grass-lands, where they needed to run fast across hard, uneven ground. And they didn't need to grasp things or spread their weight over soft wet marshes. As a result, a single hoof fit the bill.

Except . . . those missing toes are really still there, kind of. On every horse's leg under the skin are two tiny bones called "splint bones." They do little weight-bearing but may have some function in tendon attachment.

Great Feet

Alexander the Great's horse, according to the stories, had two extra toes on each hind leg that were nonfunctional but visible. True? Who knows, but it makes for a good story.

What's the relationship between donkeys, horses, and mules?

A: *Donkeys and horses are different species,* but close enough to mate with each other. When you breed a male donkey to a female horse, you get a mule. When you reverse the recipe, you get a hinny, but most people call all horse-donkey hybrids mules, no matter the combination of parentage. Mules are more common anyway, since male horses and female donkeys don't seem to get pregnant that easily.

These hybrids are generally unable to reproduce, although in recent years they have been cloned. With their long ears, mules take after the donkey side of the family in appearance. They are strong, well suited to hard work, highly intelligent, and different to train than horses. As the need for a hardworking farm animal declined after the introduction of the tractor, mules were taken up by people who valued them for their distinctive traits. Today mules compete in most of the same kinds of sports that horses do, including racing. Although you'll never see a mule at the Kentucky Derby (we feel confident in saying), you may well find them in the opening races at your local fair.

There are mules as large as draft horses and as small as miniature horses, and come in a variety of colors. Some even have markings that testify to their ancestry of spotted horses.

Q: How is a purebred horse different from a Thoroughbred?

A: A Thoroughbred is a breed of horse primarily used for racing, although some ex-racers do find second careers as pleasure horses or even show jumpers or polo ponies (even though they're too tall to be called "ponies" anywhere except in the sport of polo).

Today's Thoroughbreds all trace their heritage back to one of three Arabian sires—the Darley Arabian, Godolphin Arabian, and Byerly Turk—who were imported to England and bred to the heavier native horses. After the breed was created and refined, the organizations overseeing racing stopped the crossbreeding, and today's racing Thoroughbreds are the result of breeding only to other Thoroughbreds.

Thoroughbred horses are often bred to other horses, most notably Arabians. These Anglo-Arabian crosses are popular enough to have their own horse registry.

A horse of any known breed is simply called a purebred horse.

Q: Does a horse know if he has won a race?

A: *They probably all do,* but the good ones are those who care if they've lost. These are the ones who, when confronted with a rival in the home stretch, dig down deeper to stay ahead at the wire. The racehorses who are chosen to pass their gifts along to future generations are those who win, and winning can be as much about desire as natural ability. Over time, those horses who possess what racing fans call "heart" have made their mark on the sport, with the result being an animal with a strong desire to win. You can see that desire when horses "hook up," matching each other stride for stride and unwilling to let each other take the lead.

When you have an individual racehorse with great physical ability and lots of heart, you have a winner, a horse who wants to win every bit as much as his jockey, trainer, and owner.

But even the smartest, most competitive horse probably doesn't know if he has won in a near–dead heat photo finish. We're guessing that in such cases, both horses figure they came out on top.

Q: I've heard the expression "Gotta piss like a racehorse." Is there something special about the way a racehorse relieves himself?

A: This is definitely a guy term, describing the most urgent level of needing bladder release. But why a racehorse?

Some think the expression is because of the practice of giving diuretics to racehorses known to be "bleeders." Bleeders rupture small blood vessels in the smallest portions of the bronchial tree and bleed into the lungs causing a telltale frothy blood to come out of their noses. If you "bleed" you don't "lead" a race as the condition is slowing. If bleeders are given diuretics before a race—you can see it marked on the racing form often with an "L" for the diuretic Lasix, in those states where it's legal—the drug reduces or stops the bleeding and the horses race faster. The diuretics also cause the horse to shed water weight and thus make them lighter and faster. With diuretics a racehorse's urine output soars.

But even horses who've never seen a track can produce an amazing amount of urine. They are often reluctant to urinate just anywhere, and once they get used to eliminating in a certain place (like their stall where they feel safe and secure), they'll often hold their urine until they arrive at the target zone.

Finally, if you've ever seen any horse urinate, you'll notice as large animals they rid themselves of a lot of urine quickly. Thus, when you "piss like a racehorse," you urinate quickly and loudly with an impressive stream. And proudly, since that, too, is a guy thing.

Q: Can horses taste the same flavors that we can?

A: *Horses do taste the same* basic flavors as humans, but they have different taste preferences than we do.

What tastes good to horses is greatly influenced by, if not completely controlled by, what they can smell. When a horse sticks his head into a bucket of feed, he can't see what he's about to eat because his eyes are on either side of his head. The first sense of an impending bite of food is its smell.

The other important difference between the horse's palate and the human one is that horses do not like as much variety as we humans do. They prefer consistency day in and day out. This preference has probably developed as a safety feature, because the anatomy and physiology of the equine digestive tract is designed for processing the same type of diet each day. Sudden changes in the equine diet can cause serious illnesses or even death.

We commonly think that horses prefer sweets, as many of us do. Everyone knows that horses like peppermints and sweet feed with molasses, right? While this may be true of some horses, this is actually more of a learned behavior. If you offer a treat, like a peppermint, to a horse who has never tasted one, he will likely refuse to eat it. He may turn his nose up to it, in fact, in a behavior called the flehmen response, which is really all about getting a better smell of your offering (see more on the flehmen response in a later question).

Palatability research has shown that horses may like several different flavors and prefer a slightly bitter flavor over sweet flavors. Raw cane molasses has a slightly bitter flavor, which is different from the sweet molasses we know.

Even when a horse likes a certain flavor, he may only like it little. Too much or too little of a particular flavor and the horse is likely to refuse to eat it.

Q: How long do horses live?

A: *Horses often live well into their twenties,* with purebreds typically having shorter life spans and crossbred horses longer ones. But with fewer horses being worked hard and more horses receiving excellent nutrition and veterinary care, horses, like people, are living longer than their ancestors.

In working horses, the first part of the body to fail is the legs. The aging horse may first limp or walk unevenly. Then the hair coat may get lighter or show gray, especially around the face. The hollows above the eyes deepen, lips hang looser, eyelids become more wrinkled, teeth wear, muscles weaken, the back sways, the belly sags, and the horse's gait is slower and stiffer.

People always like to know how old their animals are in "human years." Here is a general guide for horses:

- **Foals:** The baby and toddler stage for horses, this encompasses birth to weaning (typically four to six months). During this time their baby teeth erupt.

- **Weanlings:** Babies who have been removed from their mothers. In human terms, they're in elementary school.
- **Yearlings:** Youngsters who have reached their first birthdays and are like pre-teenagers in middle school. They are active, full of ideas, but not ready to work.
- **Young horses:** Like high school teenagers, these two- to three-year-old horses are physically mature and mentally immature, but considered trainable. They are losing their front baby teeth and getting adult incisors.
- **Young adult horses:** These three- to six-year-old horses are in the peak learning stage of life, comparable to college students. Typically, all adult teeth are in by the end of their fifth year.
- **Adult horses:** Between the ages of six and twelve, horses are like people in their late twenties to late forties, in relatively good health and enjoying work and play without the distractions of youth and the frailties of old age. These horses can enjoy life, work hard, play hard, and the mares are in their best years to have babies.
- **Middle-aged horses:** Between thirteen and nineteen years of age, horses are considered middle-aged. If

life has been good with adequate exercise (but not too much hard work), nutritious food, and great veterinary care, these are solid, mature horses—happy, safe, and easy to ride.

- **Senior horses:** Horses twenty years and above are equine senior citizens. Wise, but physically in decline, many still have a few good years left.
- **Old horses:** Any horse over thirty years of age is enjoying the golden years. Because horses don't have dentures, these horses have often worn their teeth to the point of becoming "gummers."

It's not uncommon these days to see horses in their thirties and, on occasion, in their early forties. Horses in their twenties are not necessarily ready to be retired. Perhaps they need to slow down, and some may need to lighten their carrying load, but being "long in the tooth" alone does not mean they are ready to head permanently to pasture.

Great strides (no pun intended) have been made in recent years in the care of the older horse. Additionally, human attitudes have changed regarding the older horse, with many horses being considered a pet to be cared for until the end. These things add up to a growing population of geriatric horses.

Q: **What is the world's most expensive equine purchase?**

A: *As of this writing, it's the Green Monkey,* a Thoroughbred who was purchased for an eye-popping $16 million as an unraced two-year-old in 2006. As of press time, the handsome bay remains unraced (and unbred), so for now, no one can say for sure if his potential will ever approach his price tag.

If you look at things from another angle, you could argue that the world's most valuable horse is the great Thoroughbred sire Storm Cat. Getting your mare a date with the Big Man will cost you a cool half-million.

Born in 1983, this grandson of the great Secretariat is starting to get a little old for stud duty, but since he has sired other horses who are now successfully standing stud themselves—including two sons who reside at the same stud farm—his influence will be felt for many generations to come.

Q: **Why do horses have such long faces?**

A: *The reason for the horse's long face* is to accommodate the impressive rows of teeth in the back of their mouth. Horses have two fundamental types of teeth: incisors in the front of their mouths for pulling grass and other feedstuff into their mouths, and a long set of molars on either side of their mouths to grind their food into the smallest particle size possible.

Q: Who was Charley Horse, and how did a leg injury get named after him?

A: See anybody with a Charley horse and he's typically hopping like a human pogo stick trying to work the cramp out of his leg.

Two theories bring the birth of the phrase to the baseball diamond of the late 1800s. In one, pitcher Charley "Old Hoss" Radbourn was said to suffer from cramps. Another story mentioned a horse named Charley who used to work the infield at Comiskey Park in Chicago. The fans noticed the horse walked with a limp and soon used the phrase Charley horse to describe limping ballplayers.

Either way, it's a colorful turn of phrase that brightens the English language—even if it has as much to do with baseball as with horses.

Q: **Is it true horses can't throw up? Why not?**

A: *True.* There is an anatomical variation in the horse that effectively puts a plug in puking.

The junction of the esophagus to the stomach has a very tight muscle or sphincter. Unlike other species, when the horse's stomach gets really full, it distends in such a way that the opening between the stomach and the esophagus is shut off. Think of kinking a garden hose to shut off the flow. As a result, horses can't throw up voluntarily or involuntarily even when they need to. The stomach will rupture before any contents come out.

A horse whose stomach ruptures is stressed and in pain, then suddenly acts better, even to the point of wanting to eat or graze as the debilitating pressure is relieved. For these unfortunate horses, this meal is their last one.

If a horse needs to pass gas, or something even worse, a veterinarian needs to insert a long tube up the nose and down into the stomach to relieve the pressure and fluid in the stomach. Makes leaning over the toilet not sound so bad, huh?

Q: **Is artificial insemination possible for horses, as it is for cattle and other animals?**

A: *Artificial insemination* using previously collected semen from top sires is absolutely possible in Thoroughbred racehorses from a practical standpoint. From a regulatory standpoint, when the beloved horse Barbaro's life ended, so did any possibility of his siring any offspring. That's because in the Sport of Kings, breeding has to be done under "live cover." That means both horses must be in attendance and the procedure must go on as naturally as possible when every minute of the act is attended to by people looking to ensure not only a successful mating but also that neither valuable racehorse is injured.

The broodmares, by the way, come to the stallion's place for breeding. That's one way to enable the stallion to "cover" as many mares as possible.

Putting a stallion up for stud is called "standing" him, and some top Thoroughbred stallions stand in both hemispheres! They cover mares during the Northern

Hemisphere's spring breeding season, and are then shuttled to Australia or other points south for arranged dates with even more mares.

A top Thoroughbred stallion can be bred to up to 200 mares a year. No doubt the job is tiring but highly satisfying for these valuable animals.

The insistence on "live cover" doesn't extend to all other kinds of horse-breeding. Artificial insemination is the norm, for example, in the breeding of Standardbred racehorses, the ones who pace or trot pulling a driver behind them in a cart called a "sulky." It is commonly practiced in many other breeds as well.

BLUE GETS
HIS HAPPY ENDING

While I did my share of riding in my teens and twenties, I was never really as much into horseback riding as I was into horses. When you're on a horse, you're pretty high up, and I'm not that fond of heights—even ladders make me woozy.

In my twenties, I broke my collarbone after I went over a jump alone after my horse hit the brakes. In my forties, I decided to return to riding, and after my first fall going over a low fence, I realized that another broken collarbone would make it pretty hard for me to write for a living. My riding is now pretty much behind me—aside from a sedate trail ride now and then—but my love of horses has never waned.

In recent years, I've become a dedicated follower of Thoroughbred horse racing.

Horse racing is business. And although most in the business truly do love horses, there are casualties that make any horse-loving fan like me wonder how she can love the sport. After all, in the eight months following his Preakness disaster, when Barbaro was given every chance to live, dozens of other horses were put down with injuries that weren't as severe. To the bottom line–minded, saving the horses at the bottom of the racing hierarchy—"cheap claimers" in race-track parlance—just doesn't pencil out.

Which is why the story of Bluesthestandard stands out for me as a model of the best of what can happen when those in racing show how much they care.

Blue was one of my most favorite racehorses, a modestly bred horse (bred in Georgia, in fact) who rose up through the ranks to the point where he actually finished second in one of the top races of the year, at the 2003 Breeders' Cup.

And then, he headed back down.

A couple of years later at the Del Mar Thoroughbred Club near San Diego, I was there as Blue was pulled up in a lower-level race with an injury and vanned off the track. He didn't die that day, but his fortunes didn't get much better.

He came back at an even lower level, not far from the very bottom ranks of racing, with little hope for the future. Trainer Kristin Mulhall decided enough was enough. She arranged to take ownership of the horse and retired him to her training farm.

A few months went by, and I heard nothing about Blue. And then I got an e-mail from Mulhall herself, who'd noticed that I had mentioned Blue on my website.

"I just wanted to let you know that Blue is as happy as can be and is absolutely spoiled rotten," she wrote. "He has the most personality of any horse I've ever been around . . . I couldn't part with him if someone offered me a million dollars. He will be a part of the family for the rest of his life."

Blue's happy ending isn't shared by all race-horses, or even by most of them. That's why several nonprofits work to rehabilitate and place washed-up racehorses. Some of these horses can be trained to be show jumpers, others as trail horses. Some can only be placed as pets because their injuries no longer allow them to be ridden.

I've long supported these organizations financially, and when I finally get that bit of land I've always dreamed of, you can be sure I'll be calling one of them to offer a "forever home" to a former racer who just needs a soft spot to land for the rest of his days.

Gina Spadafori

Q: Is it fair to ride police horses on noisy, scary city streets?

A: *Police horses do have a tough job.* They are asked to deal with rioting crowds, gunfire, and the noise and chaos of city traffic. No police horse is asked to tolerate this kind of stuff without considerable training, however. Police horses are taught to deal with situations that would scare the stuffing out of an ordinary horse.

Before a horse can become a police mount, the animal has to undergo a temperament test. The horse is evaluated to make sure he has the kind of personality that can tolerate the kind of stressors that are part of a police horse's daily life. The horse is then desensitized to loud noises, crowds, and many other types of stimuli, such as an umbrella opening under the horse's nose. Several months of training are involved before the horse is ready to get out there and do the job with an officer on board.

The payoff for all this hard work is excellent care and a cushy retirement. Many major cities have police horse retirement farms, where police horses who can no longer work spend the rest of their lives. Smaller cities sometimes place their retired police horses in good homes or give them to the officers who rode them during their careers.

Q: How big is a horse's brain? What's the ratio of a horse's brain compared to other animals?

A: *Horse lore says a horse's brain* is about the size of his testicle. Speaking more scientifically, a horse's brain is on average about 20 ounces. The human brain weighs more than twice that, while a great white shark's brain weighs less than 2 ounces and a house cat's about an ounce.

To be even more precise, the average horse's brain (taking all breeds into account) ranges from 19.4 to 27.16 ounces. Not that it matters, really, since one of our experts told us the true measure of equine intelligence: When you think a horse is stupid, he'll outsmart you! When you think he is smart, he'll be stupid as a rock!

Q: **What does it mean when a horse pulls his upper lip up and inhales?**

A: *Put a stallion together with a mare* and you may see a funny face. In a strange behavior called the flehmen response, the stallion curls his top lip, exposing his upper teeth and gums. Horses sometimes go through similar facial contortions in response to other smells besides mare urine, including odors they don't like, such as horse dewormer.

The curled lip effectively closes off the nostrils (like a swimmer's nose plugs) and traps the fragrance inside the nasal cavity. Like adjusting your car's heating and air-conditioning system so it recirculates the air, in the flehmen response, the trapped scent goes to specialized organs that are supersensitive at detecting minute details of pheromones (a chemical secreted that influences the behavior or development of others of the same species, often functioning as a sexual attractant). The pheromones tell the supersniffer details such as sex, sexual status (sterilized, in heat), recently exercised, emotional status (stressed, happy), and also make it possible for horses to identify each other as individuals. Humans have social security numbers and fingerprints; horses have unique scents.

Back to the flehmen response. Simultaneously with the cartoonish sniff, the stallion rubbernecks, telescoping his head from his body, and takes a strong whiff of what would appear to be the most tantalizing scent in the world.

While the smell of urine doesn't do much for humans, for horses the complex orchestration of movement and expression in the flehmen response visibly shows great interest in the fragrance of the female and may be a harbinger of the proverbial "roll in the hay."

In the equine version of girl-on-girl action, the intoxicating chemicals in the urine may also cause a mare to perform "the face."

Q: **Does the hair on the lower legs of Clydesdales have a purpose, or is it strictly decorative?**

A: When the draft horses that were the ancestors of today's Clydesdale were first bred centuries ago in Europe, farmers favored horses with a lot of hair on their lower legs. It seemed this hair helped protect the horses' legs from scratches and cuts as the animals worked in the field.

Today, this hair, called "feather," is sought after for other reasons. Horses with a lot of feather are considered more attractive in the show ring. It's easy to see why: as the horse moves, the feather ripples in the breeze, giving the horse the look that he is floating.

Feather is a genetically recessive trait, which means in order to get a horse with feathering on his feet, both of the horse's parents had to have it as well.

Other breeds besides the Clydesdale have abundant feathering as well. The Shire, Gypsy Vanner Horse, and Friesian are just a few of the feather breeds.

Q: **Why do horses have such big nostrils?**

A: To understand a horse's nostrils, you might want to compare a Formula One racing car to a gas-sipping economy car. Horses, who until a hundred years ago were the only thing available for a fast ride, were built for speed. Speed came from thin legs with muscles high up in the body, high-pumping cardiovascular systems, huge lungs (cows, by contrast, have tiny lungs), and big nostrils that could flare if needed to scoop in more air.

Think of the huge, flared nostrils on a racing horse like the hood scoop or supercharger blower on a powerful machine pushing air to the engine. In a horse, the nostrils pull incredible amounts of air into the lungs to fuel a race away from predators, out of the racetrack gate, or in a pasture, racing the wind toward the fence for a molasses treat.

Q: **What, exactly, is "a horse of a different color"?**

A: *"A horse of a different color"* means "unlike the subject at hand."

Horses are registered at birth, and the documentation includes not only the foal's mother and father but a record of their colors and markings. When a horse is traded or sold, the registration is transferred and the markings checked. A "horse of a different color" than the one listed on the registration is bound to raise eyebrows.

All might be in order, though. Mother Nature does play tricks with color as a horse matures. Like Dalmatians (born without spots) and human babies (born with blue eyes), over time horses can change as well. Luckily, with today's advances in animal identification, including DNA testing, you can do a little genetic testing, so not just the horse's hairdresser will know for sure.

Q: How do they get racehorses from Europe to North America and back?

A: Top-dollar horses such as racehorses and world-class show jumpers travel the equine equivalent of first class, with the help of a handful of companies that move such valuable animals routinely. One of those companies may surprise you: it's not uncommon for FedEx to ship horses, although we're guessing you can't just drop yours off at the local office.

Horses are loaded onto planes in one of two ways. Sometimes they walk up a large ramp into the cargo hold and a "standing stall" is built around them. More commonly, they are put into separate crates that a crane lifts and places into the plane's cargo hold. The animals can be sedated, but most submit to the unusual process with no more than a curious look-around. Attendants travel with the horses and each horse has his own water and hay. The whole process of intercontinental travel can run as high as $30,000.

Although they don't have to take off their horseshoes after waiting in security lines to board a plane, horses are subject to stringent biosecurity precautions. Horses arriving in the United States can land at only three ports of entry—Newburgh, New York; Miami, Florida; or Los Angeles, California—and they have to be quarantined both before and after their arrival. Once in the States, the horses are inspected by veterinarians, sprayed for parasites, and have blood samples collected from them.

Horses leaving the United States must have several blood tests and vaccinations that are determined by their final destination. Quarantines are the norm for these horses, too.

Q: Why do some horses wear blankets? Do they need them to stay warm?

A: *Horses generate a lot of heat.* They're herbivores, like cattle and deer, and that means they have to have a way to get nutrients from the cellulose in plants. They accomplish this amazing feat with the aid of bacteria. In the horse, these bacteria are housed in the cecum. The horse eats the plant material, the bacteria digest the cellulose, and the horse lives off the breakdown products from the bacteria. What a great system, huh?

The bacteria in the horse produces another interesting byproduct: heat. Horses have what amounts to a plant-digesting furnace in their guts, and that helps to keep them warm. Horses also position themselves for best protection against the elements, facing their ample rumps into the wind and rain.

This doesn't mean some horses can't use a nice blanket now and then. While many horses are acclimated to cold weather and can do well in their fuzzy winter coats without blankets, those animals who spend most of their time protected by stalls need extra warmth when they go out to pasture.

In the summer, you'll often see horses in blankets, but it's not for warmth. These lightweight garments are "fly sheets," intended to protect the animal against nature's most annoying equine pest.

Q: What is a horse's "chestnut"?

A: Chestnuts are callous like objects on the inside of legs, just above the knee on the front legs and below the hock on the rear ones. The chestnut is an evolutionary remnant, thought to be the remainder of what on a dog would be a foot pad. Remember, horses—or the animals from which the modern horse developed—originally had five toes. Over time, the two outer toes disappeared completely, the next two shrank to almost invisible status alongside the leg bones, and the middle became the hoof, with the protective hard case of the hoof approximately equal to our fingernails (and made of the same material).

The chestnuts, and another vestigial structure called the ergot, remain with no purpose except perhaps to remind us of the many-toed creature the horse once was.

Q: **How many bones does a horse have?**

A: *Most horses have 205, but not all.* The Arabian differs from most other horses in the structure of the ribs and vertebrae. Instead of the usual eighteen ribs and six lumbar vertebrae, Arabians have seventeen ribs and five lumbar vertebrae. Some Spanish Mustangs also have five lumbar vertebrae.

The bones of a horse not only provide a frame for the muscles and the tendons to produce motion, but they also protect their internal organs. Bones are held firmly together by ligaments, which allow movement but also prevent overextension of the joints.

Q: Where did horses originate?

A: *Although we see humans and horses* in a partnership, life wasn't always that way for us. Early humans hunted horses for food. These animals evolved in North America, then crossed over the Bering Strait and spread through Asia and Europe during the Ice Age.

About 10,000 years ago, horse migration ceased as the horse became extinct in the Americas. Anthropologists suspect horses were hunted to extinction here by early humans.

On the other side of the world, horses were becoming domesticated. There's evidence that this first took place in what is now the Ukraine, where people lived by herding horses and cattle some 6,000 years ago. At the same time in ancient Egypt and Arabia, the wild ass was being tamed.

These animals were not ridden at first, but rather used to pull a cart. When Europeans found their way to the Americas, the riding of horses was well established. And soon, the horse was reestablished in the land where he first began.

The First Horse Tattoo

Branding on horses has been used as proof of ownership for more than 2,000 years.

Q: Why do horses walk and poop at the same time?

A: *Partly because they have to go,* but also because they're nervous. Horses defecate frequently when nervous, but they need to be relaxed to urinate normally. What's the difference?

The autonomic nervous system controls basic body functions and is made up of two opposing parts, the sympathetic and the parasympathetic systems. The sympathetic system takes over in upsetting circumstances, causing the release of adrenaline, which in turn revs up the body for action. As part of this display, the gut gets moving and so do the bowels. Lighten the load, you might have to run!

When the alarm is over, the parasympathetic system takes charge and settles everything down. It's at this relaxed point that a horse will say, "aaahhhhh," and release his urine.

Q: Why is a smart person said to have "horse sense"?

A: The favorite line we ran across in our research is actually an old joke: "Horse sense is what keeps horses from betting on people."

Humor aside, "horse sense" is practical knowledge, as opposed to, say, "book learning." A more urban way of putting it might be "street smarts."

Think back to the days when buying a horse suitable for work might mean the difference between success and failure. A horse trader just wants to sell the horse, and if you're stupid enough to buy one who's not capable of doing the job—no matter how good he looks on paper—then you're going to get taken.

But if you have a practical knowledge of the pitfalls of horse-buying and how to get the horse you need at a reasonable price, then you have "horse smarts." And you'll also have a good horse. As another wag puts it, "Horse sense is stable thinking and the ability to say nay!"

Q: How do horses keep from overheating?

A: *When it's hot,* humans turn on the air-conditioning, dogs pant, and pigs wallow. Horses do none of the above and manage to stay relatively cool. How? They sweat.

Horses sweat from the whole surface of their skin, but the highest concentration of sweat glands can be found in the neck, chest, shoulders, and flanks.

During exercise, energy is released in the form of muscle movement and heat. This heat has to be removed or internal organs can be damaged. The evaporation of sweat off the skin absorbs and dissipates this potentially harmful heat. It's not the sweat that cools the horse, but the evaporation.

A "Hot" Tip for the Track

When a racehorse sweats profusely on the way to the starting gate on a day when hot weather can't be blamed, bettors worry that the animal is too stressed to race well. They say the horse looks "washed-out," and will be inclined to put their money elsewhere.

Q: I once heard that all racehorses are born on January 1. How is that possible?

A: *On paper, all Northern Hemisphere* racehorses are born on January 1. In reality, they're born when they're ready to be born, and there's not much that can be done to change that. That means if a foal pops out on December 31, he officially turns a year old within his first twenty-four hours of life.

Why? To keep things nice and tidy when it comes to racing. All Thoroughbred racehorses have an official January 1 birthday to make it possible to classify horses for age-related events such as the Kentucky Derby, a race for three-year-olds only. (In the Southern Hemisphere, the official birthday for racehorses is August 1.)

It's pretty obvious that a foal born early in the year has an advantage over one born later in the spring, when they all have to compete against each other as equals. A foal born late in the year will have a hard time maturing quickly enough to have any hope of winning the top races for three-year-olds against horses who may be months older. That's why Thoroughbred breeders begin their official breeding activities on February 15 of each year to produce foals as near to January 1 of the following year as possible—just not before, they hope!

"Late foals" may not make the Run for the Roses, but they do bloom in their own time. You'll see some of them pop up at races later in the year, not for the first Saturday in May at the Kentucky Derby, but for later races on the circuit. Top among them: the Travers Stakes, the oldest Thoroughbred race in the United States and a key race for three-year-olds every summer. It's one of the marquee events at the historic Saratoga Racetrack in upstate New York.

Q: Do horses ever give birth to twins? Triplets?

A: About one in 10,000 horse pregnancies results in twins, but only 20 percent of these survive. As for triplets, you're about as likely to spot Bigfoot as to see the birth of healthy horse triplets from a single mare.

While getting multiples out alive is a rare occasion, you can spot them if you look early with an ultrasound. Thoroughbred mares conceive twins 15 to 25 percent of the time, and triplets now and then. But the march of time isn't kind to the siblings as the pregnancy continues.

When the twins implant in the same horn of the uterus, the mare's system will reduce the pregnancy to a single foal. If, however, they implant in separate uterine horns, twin foals may very well develop and grow until about the ninth month of an eleven-month gestation period, at which time they spontaneously abort. There just isn't enough room or blood supply to provide enough nutrition for two babies. One baby will get "starved out" and die, which typically causes abortion of the other baby, even though that one is healthy.

Occasionally the starved fetus will become "mummified," meaning the embryo died and the mare's body was able to wall it off, preventing any dead tissue toxins from hurting the other fetus or causing abortion. Usually these foals are born premature because the mummy still took up space. In these freakish deliveries, the mummified fetus is delivered last, and is as strange a thing as you'd ever want to see.

If twins do make it on the ground alive, the odds are stacked against them both, at least in the wild. Remember, predators are waiting, and two foals are at a disadvantage when it comes to being able to get enough milk to grow quickly and learn herd behaviors for protection.

Among domestic horses, sometimes multiples are divided early in utero and placed in "wombs for rent" in other mares. If everything goes right, the result can be twins, triplets, or even quadruplets who have never met each other.

Q: Do racehorses have bigger hearts than other horses?

A: Racetrack intuition would bet on "yes," since we've been breeding racehorses to run longer and faster for centuries and one would assume that would naturally select for bigger pumps to power a horse to cross the line first.

In fact, great racehorses do indeed have larger hearts, and this was one of the reasons that Secretariat was so successful. His heart was reported to weigh approximately 22 pounds, compared to a normal heart weight of 10 to12 pounds. Australia's most famous racehorse, Phar Lap, born in 1926, was noted for his large 14-pound heart. Historical records dating long before either of these bighearted horses were born point to the exceptional racehorse Eclipse; in fact, the racing industry's annual awards are named after him and make note of his larger-than-normal heart.

People who buy and sell racehorses think hearts are important, and it's fairly routine for these horses to have an ultrasound check performed by a veterinary cardiologist. A large heart won't make up for poor conformation or lameness problems, of course, and it's just one aspect of the physical attributes that a great racehorse needs.

Of course, there's heart and then there's *heart.* Many a racehorse with normal physical attributes can rise above it all with his desire to make it to the finish line first.

Q: Can you neuter or spay a horse like you would a dog or a cat?

A: *The neutering of male horses is fairly routine.* The procedure is called "gelding," as are the horses after the surgery. (One of the most famous geldings in recent years is Kentucky Derby winner Funny Cide.) Veterinarians also call the surgery castration, a word that seems difficult for the layman (and we do mean "man") to say without wincing.

Horses are gelded more for behavior than for birth control. Stallions can be difficult to handle and often dangerous to be around; once gelded, these horses calm down and become much easier to ride and live with.

Most people choose to castrate a colt before his second birthday, as this is when the hormones kick in (literally and figuratively), and the horse can become as unruly as a young man at a beer party. In the bad old days, for both the horse and the surgeon, a horse was cinched down with ropes and operated on without anesthesia. Today, castration can be done standing or lying down, with proper medication to ensure that they don't feel a thing.

A curious side effect of castration is that geldings tend to be taller than stallions as a result of removing the major source of testosterone, which exerts an effect on the growth plates in the long bones of the legs. This is the reason why many stallions have a stockier, compact build, like those human bodybuilders you see prancing around in their muscle shirts.

Okay, so what about the females? Yes, they can be spayed, but that's "ovariectomized" in veterinary parlance, and it's far less common than gelding. The procedure is typically done only if a mare has ovarian tumors, a severely diseased reproductive tract, or for behavioral problems (brazen horse hussies). The procedure has more recently been made easier through use of a laparoscope and is done on a standing mare through her flank, just behind the rib cage. While in a dog and cat you take out the ovaries and the uterus through an abdominal incision, in a horse only the ovaries are removed.

While most equine reproductive surgeries are for behavior or health reasons, it should also be noted that some horse rescue groups encourage spaying mares prior to adopting them out as a way to decrease the unwanted horse population.

Seeing Spots

In North America, the first documented case of a regular gelding program was with the Indians of the Palouse region, whose snip-snip program was aimed at optimizing the chances of getting the characteristics they were after in their horses, the famed Appaloosa or spotted horse, which was named after this region of the Pacific Northwest.

Q: What is it like to be hung like a horse?

A: *When puffed-chest men* are joking around about the size of their "equipment," they often say, "I'm hung like a horse." But when the beer stops talking and these same studs start walking out of the shower, we know many of them are, in fact, hung like sea horses. But we digress.

Are horses that big, relatively speaking, or are their members large because they are? Do different-sized horses (Clydesdale vs. Quarter Horse vs. pony vs. miniature horse) have different-sized equipment? Can two horses from the same mother and father sport dramatically different members, with one horse in the Penile Hall of Fame and the other in the Hall of Shame?

Although the horse penis is long, other animals, such as cattle or llamas, have even longer penises. The average stallion penis is about 60 to 80 cm (about 24 to 32 inches) long and 10 to 15 cm (about 4 to 6 inches) in diameter in the erect state. An erect organ is about 2 to 2.5 times larger than a flaccid one.

There is a certain relationship between the size of the breed and size of the penis. In general, draft horses are larger than pleasure horses, who are larger than ponies, who are larger than miniature breeds. The difference is not nearly as noticeable between individuals in the same category. For example, Arabian horses are about the same as Thoroughbreds. But like "The Little Engine That Could," of all the *Equus*, donkeys are the biggest.

A respected veterinary theriogenologist (the branch of veterinary medicine that deals with reproduction in all its aspects) we interviewed for this book reported that he's recently examined a gelding at the veterinary school clinic with an abnormally small penis (about one-third the normal size). The main complaint was that the horse had urine scalds on the inside of the thighs because the penis couldn't protrude during urination. Rather than a normal stream of urine, it was more a gurgling yellow spring that ran down the horse's legs.

Oh my, the shame of having four hooves and the ability to neigh without being hung like a horse!

Q: Why can't they save horses who break a leg? Why can't they just put a cast on it?

A: *Even in the best circumstances*—a young, healthy horse and a talented, experienced equine orthopedic surgeon—horse fractures are not easy to fix. A horse is a large, heavy animal whose weight is supported by four very slender legs, which is a good design for running, but not for standing still and recuperating from an injury.

In the old days, a horse with a broken leg was always treated the same way: with a merciful bullet to the brain. Today as long as the fracture isn't too severe (sometimes the bone explodes into hundreds of pieces and is irreparable), the budget isn't too small (the cost of some equine orthopedic repairs will cause the horse owner's legs to buckle), or the expectation too great (perhaps the injured horse can become a trail or pasture horse but can no longer race or be a hunter-jumper), equine veterinarians have a lot of options in treating broken bones.

But the truth is many horses with broken legs do get

put down every day, although it's usually with the help of a veterinarian, not a gun like you'd see in a Western movie. Many a horse loaded gently onto a horse ambulance at the racetrack or rodeo is headed for a date with the needle, out of the view of the spectators, who cannot bear seeing the final drama unfold in front of them. (For horses who cannot be loaded onto the ambulance, a screen is quickly raised between horse and grandstand.)

Sometimes the decision to put down a horse is economical—the cost of care exceeds the value the horse would have after mending. But many times the injury is so severe that even all the money, time, and great veterinary minds in the world cannot save the animal, a point recently underscored by the heroic and ultimately unsuccessful fight to save the Kentucky Derby winner Barbaro.

There are really two problems when dealing with a horse with a broken leg. One is the fracture. Where is it? If it's in the joint, it's worse. How bad is it? A simple fracture with a clean break is a serious injury. A comminuted fracture (one with many pieces) or a compound fracture where the bone has protruded from the skin, greatly increasing the risk of infection, is a very serious injury.

If the decision is made to fix a broken leg, the veterinarian may use splints, casts, or internal fixes with various plates, screws, interlocking nails, and other orthopedic devices. The horse is usually put on painkillers and seda-tives and prescribed stall rest. Sometimes the horses are put in slings to keep part of the weight off the affected limb.

The other problem is the recovery. Horses are designed to spend their lives in motion. Many don't react well to the confinement and convalescence necessary to heal. Tap-dancing, Hi-Ho-Silvering, stall-kicking horses with broken legs aren't likely candidates for weeks and months of confinement and treatment.

Even with a seemingly successful orthopedic repair and a compliant patient, things can go wrong. After all, it wasn't the fracture that ultimately led to the loss of Barbaro, but rather problems with other legs that had to take on greater weight-bearing, a situation that led to a hoof disease called laminitis (a separation of the wall from the underlying structures of the hoof). Some horses don't tolerate confinement, and others develop infections or intolerance to medications.

Economic realities aside, a horse with a broken leg and a long list of complicating issues, facing a long and chal-lenging repair with a high likelihood of complications, is probably not going to make it, no matter how hard every-one tries.

For these animals, ending the suffering is the only compassionate choice.

A Better Track

In recent years, the Thoroughbred horse-racing industry has looked to provide safer track surfaces with the goal of saving both horses and jockeys from severe injuries. These synthetic track surfaces are made up of materials that include polypropylene fibers, recycled rubber, and silica sand covered in a wax coating. They provide a surface that can be raced on in all but the worst weather conditions, with more cushioning for the relatively fragile legs of racehorses.

While the move toward cushioned tracks predated the Barbaro tragedy, there's no doubt that the Derby winner's much-followed injury and ultimate loss of life has hastened the racing industry's interest in making tracks safer for horses, jockeys, exercise riders, and a horse-loving public that doesn't want to see these beautiful animals die for its entertainment.

Q: **Is it true veterinarians do acupuncture, chiropractic, and other alternative treatments on horses?**

A: *Besides using proverbial "horse pills,"* syringes full of medicines, and tubes full of healthy gunk destined for the horse's innards, veterinarians are increasingly practicing "integrative" medicine—a blend of Eastern and Western care.

Cue the incense and mood music here as the veterinarian prepares to help heal the horse with acupuncture, chiropractic, Reiki, reflexology, massage, homeopathy, herbal remedies, and aromatherapy. These integrative medicine techniques don't just make the owner feel good and bulge the pockets of ex-hippies turned veterinarians; they indeed hold great benefits for many horses.

As practiced today, the ancient Chinese skill of acupuncture is well accepted both by the horses (they don't seem to mind the needles) and the owners, who see benefits for their animals. Although exactly how acupuncture works isn't completely understood, the practice does show benefits for many animals.

Equine chiropractic patients can't lay facedown on a bed and get their backs cracked. Instead, equine chiropractors—often veterinarians specializing in chiropractic—come to their patients and stand on a stool while they apply pressure to appropriate places along the equine spine.

Equine chiropractors address issues such as lameness, sore backs, and stiff necks—pretty much the same stuff human chiropractors deal with. Horses often enjoy their visits with the chiropractor, with some practically falling asleep while the chiropractor works.

Each state has its own laws as to who can perform these modalities of veterinary practice, whether it's a licensed veterinarian or a layperson working with a licensed veterinarian.

Q: **Are there really hairpieces for horses?**

A: *What do you do if you're a horse* and Mother Nature cheated you in the hair department? You can't do a coast-to-coast comb-over or get a prescription for a hair transplant, but you can get a hairpiece. Or rather, your owner can, because a horse really couldn't care less.

People who show their horses care plenty, which is why there's a lot of money in making horses look hairier in all the right places. You can find companies who produce either natural horse hair or extruded fiber hairpieces that can be formed to make a long mane, tail, or forelock or that can supplement horses who have thinner hair than desired. These hairpieces are available in any color, thickness, or length and are fitted with small attachments that are braided or glued into the existing tailbone and hair of the horse.

The artificial hair, matched to the color of the real stuff, is mingled and groomed into the natural fall and voilà, a lovely, full head or tail of hair—at least from twenty feet away!

But let's say you don't want to botch your horse's hairdo as badly as your own. You'll, of course, hire the hairdresser to come and not only place the wigs appropriately, but also shine up, straighten or crimp, weave or braid the real hair so that the whole picture is complete. Most breed associations allow this "natural" embellishment, and the show horses that are so polished are a vision indeed.

As a measure of how big the horse beauty business is, we know of a person who made $30,000 in three weeks braiding horses' manes and tails during show season. She had bleeding fingers and almost no sleep, but that kind of money isn't horse feed!

Q: Do you guys ever get tired of giving advice on animals every day of your lives until the end of time?

A: *Of course not.* It's either do this or get real jobs. How many jobs are there in this world where every single day of your life you can make someone else's life a little better just by sharing your love of animals and your hard-earned knowledge of how to make living with them easier?

Not many, huh? Truthfully, we consider ourselves lucky and more than a little bit blessed.

And that, as they say, is our final answer.

Acknowledgments

This book and its two companions would not have been possible without the generosity of many top veterinarians and other equine experts who were gracious in providing their expertise. It's exciting and inspiring for us to know and be able to share ideas with such an outstanding group of professionals, brilliant and caring people who have dedicated their careers to improving the lives of horses and the people who love them.

We want to take the time to thank them all, including: Dr. Mark Baus of Fairfield Equine Associates in Newtown, Connecticut; Dr. Gilbert Burns, associate professor of anatomy at the College of Veterinary Medicine at Washington State University; Dr. Rick DeBowes, professor of equine surgery, associate dean for Development and External Relations, and director of Professionalism and Medical Life Skills Programs at the College of Veterinary Medicine at Washington State University (Dr.

DeBowes is the instructor who foolishly let Dr. Becker pass the equine block in veterinary school and gave him marginally enough knowledge to pass the boards); Dr. Tim Ellis, Mid Rivers Equine Center in Wentzville, Missouri; Ben Haggin of Reynolds-Bell Thoroughbred Services in Lexington, Kentucky (Mr. Haggin's direct ancestor, James Ben Ali Haggin, won the Kentucky Derby in 1886 with a horse named Ben Ali. You can look it up!); Dr. Katherine Albro Houpt, James Law Professor of Animal Behavior, College of Veterinary Medicine at Cornell University; Dr. Karen Hayes, www.integral-horse.com; Dr. Lisa Jacobsen, Big Sky Equine Veterinary Services and member of the Montana State University Equine Science Advisory Board, Clyde Park, Montana; Dr. Scott King of Purina Mills and host of *Animal Makeover* on RFD-TV; Rick Lamb, host of *The Horse Show with Rick Lamb* on RFD-TV and author of three horse books, including *Human to Horsemanship–Roadmap for a Life-Changing Journey;* Dr. Marie L. Meschke, Sandpoint, Idaho; Dr. Robert Miller, www.robertmiller.com; Dr. Cherise Neu, Sandpoint, Idaho; Dr. Cheryl Rahal, Phoenix, Arizona; Dr. Rhonda Rathgeber, Hagyard Equine Medical Institute, Lexington, Kentucky; Dr. John Schotman, Lake Wales Veterinary Clinic, Lake Wales, Florida; James Spencer, horse specialist with the Nez

Perce Tribe, Lapwai, Idaho; Dr. Kim Sprayberry, assistant editor, American Veterinary Medical Association; Dr. Ahmed Tibary, associate professor of theriogenology, College of Veterinary Medicine at Washington State University; Dr. Kathy Trimpi, Roanoke Valley Equine Center, Daleville, Virginia; Dr. Jim Waldsmith, San Luis Obispo, California, Dr. Kim L. Ward, Martensville, Saskatchewan; and Dr. Jeffrey Young, Young Veterinary Services, Amarillo, Texas. We also want to acknowledge the support and help of our publisher, Peter Vegso, owner of the Vegso Racing Stables in Ocala, Florida.

On a more personal level, we simple cannot do what we do without the support of our family and friends. We love you.

Thanks to all the folks at Health Communications, Inc., who saw the promise of this book and gave us the go-ahead to write together and have a great time doing so. Of all the great folks at HCI, we'd especially like to thank our editor Allison Janse for her hard work.

Teresa and Dr. Marty Becker
Audrey Pavia
Gina Spadafori

Special Thanks

The authors acknowledge the above-and-beyond contribution of our technical editor, Dr. Karen Hayes.

Hayes is the award-winning author of seven horse-care books and hundreds of magazine articles and is a frequent lecturer in standing-room-only lecture halls at horse expositions.

Hayes earned her bachelor's degree in biology in 1975, and her DVM degree in 1979 from the University of Illinois, where the faculty honored her with the Upjohn Award for proficiency in Large Animal Clinical Medicine—the first woman in the history of the college to win this award. She worked in private practice for several years, then joined the faculty at the veterinary college at the University of Wisconsin-Madison, where she conducted research and earned a postdoctoral master's degree in equine reproduction. She then returned to clinical practice.

A lifelong horsewoman, Hayes continues to write and lecture. Her passion these days is to stimulate a grassroots educational movement to better the lives of horses and their caretakers and to help horse facilities make a smaller footprint on the earth. To that end, she created www. integralhorse.com, a free educational website full of downloadable lectures about horse care and horse keeping. Two new topics are posted every month, and over time the archives have become a significant source for rock-solid information that's practical and logical, but not particularly well known in the horse world, which tends to do things a certain way just because that's the way it's "always" been done.

We cannot thank her enough for her help with this book.

Do You Have a Question?

We know you have more than 101 questions about horses! So we're already planning another book to answer even more of your questions.

Would you like your question answered in the next book? Drop us a line at askaboutpets@gmail.com, or contact us through our PetConnection.com website. We're looking forward to your questions.

About the Authors

Dr. Marty Becker and Teresa Becker

As a veterinarian, media personality, author, and educator, Dr. Marty Becker has become known as the "best-loved family doctor for pets."

Dr. Becker is the popular veterinary contributor to ABC-TV's *Good Morning, America.* In association with the American Animal Hospital Association, Dr. Becker also hosts a nationally syndicated radio program, *Top Vets Talk Pets,* on the Health Radio Network. He has coauthored two previous books with Gina Spadafori, *Why Do Cats Always Land on Their Feet?* and the *New York Times* bestseller, *Why Do Dogs Drink Out of the Toilet?* The two also write a weekly pet-care feature for newspapers across the United States and Canada, syndicated by Universal Press.

He has appeared on *Animal Planet* and is a frequent guest on national network and cable TV and radio shows. Dr. Becker is an adjunct professor at both his alma mater, the Washington State University College of Veterinary Medicine, and at the Colorado State University College of Veterinary Medicine. Additionally, he has lectured at every veterinary school in the United States and has been named Companion Animal Veterinarian of the Year by the Delta Society and the American Veterinary Medical Association.

Dr. Becker is coauthor of the fastest-selling pet book in history, *Chicken Soup for the Pet Lover's Soul*, and is either sole author or coauthor of other top-selling books, including other animal books in the Chicken Soup line, *The Healing Power of Pets: Harnessing the Amazing Ability of Pets to Make and Keep People Happy and Healthy,* and *Fitness Unleashed: A Dog and Owner's Guide to Losing Weight and Gaining Health Together!*

Teresa Becker was born and raised in northern Idaho and enjoyed an idyllic childhood riding horses at every opportunity. A schoolteacher by profession, Teresa received her master's degree in sports administration and taught in elementary schools in Twin Falls, Idaho, for many years. As an adult, Teresa rode Western pleasure in Quarter Horse shows, but now her ideal day involves trail riding her palomino, Gabriel. She is the coauthor of *Chicken Soup for the Horse Lover's Soul* and *Chicken Soup for the Horse Lover's Soul II.*

The Beckers have two children, daughter Mikkel and son Lex. The family shares their Almost Heaven Ranch in northern Idaho with two dogs, five barn cats, and four Quarter Horses—Gabriel, Glo Lopin, Pegasus, and Sugar Babe.

Audrey Pavia

Audrey Pavia is a former editor of *Horse Illustrated* magazine and an award-winning freelance writer specializing in equine subjects. She is the author of several horse books, including *Horses for Dummies* and *Trail Riding: A Complete Guide*. Audrey has also authored hundreds of articles on various equine topics in a number of horse publications, including *Western Horseman, The Trail Rider, Equestrian Retailer, Horses USA, Appaloosa Journal, Paint Horse Journal, Quarter Horses USA, Equine Veterinary Management,* and *USDF Connection* magazines.

In addition to her experience as an equine writer, she is also a former managing editor of *Dog Fancy* magazine and a former senior editor of the *American Kennel Club Gazette*. She has authored more than 700 articles on the subject of animals and has written several books on various kinds of pets.

Audrey has been involved with horses since the age of nine, has owned and cared for horses throughout her life, and has trained in both Western and English disciplines. She currently resides in Southern California with her husband, Randy Mastronicola, a Spanish Mustang named Milagro, a Quarter Horse named Red, and critters of all kinds, including Nigel the trick-performing Pembroke Welsh Corgi, one of the few animals who has ever managed to upstage Dr. Becker on a TV show.

Gina Spadafori

Gina Spadafori has been blessed with the opportunity to combine two of her dearest loves—animals and words—into a career writing about animals. Since 1984, she has authored an award-winning weekly column on pets and their care, which now appears in newspapers across the United States and Canada through the Universal Press Syndicate.

She and Dr. Marty Becker joined forces in 2006, working together not only on a new syndicated pet-care feature for Universal, but also on the *New York Times* bestseller *Why Do Dogs Drink Out of the Toilet?* as well as *Why Do Cats Always Land on Their Feet?*

Gina has served on the board of directors for both the Cat Writers' Association (CWA) and the Dog Writers Association of America (DWAA). She is a recipient of the DWAA's Maxwell Medallion for the best newspaper column, and her column has also been honored with a certificate of excellence by the CWA. The first edition of her top-selling book *Dogs for Dummies* was given the President's Award for the best writing on dogs and the Maxwell Medallion for the best general reference work, both by the DWAA.

Along with coauthor Dr. Paul D. Pion, a top veterinary cardiologist, she was given the CWA's awards for the best work on feline nutrition, best work on feline behavior, and best work on responsible cat care for the top-selling *Cats for Dummies*. The book was also named one of the hundred best feline moments in the twentieth century by *Cat Fancy* magazine. With internationally recognized avian specialist Dr. Brian L. Speer, she has also written *Birds for Dummies,* one of the best-selling books on pet birds ever written. Her books have been translated into many languages, including French, Serbian, Danish, Japanese, and Russian.

Gina lives in northern California in a decidedly multi-species home.

More from America's Favorite Vet